Dylan Thomas's early ad
mesmerized by the music of
while his detractors found
and plunge of his work only
In the past few   It...... controversy '

theless to create, and to exorcize the
powers of darkness with gaiety, fancy,
and wit.

Among the essays collected in this volume are:

The Poetry of Dylan Thomas
DAVID DAICHES

The Welsh Background
JOHN ACKERMAN

Dylan Thomas's Play for Voices
RAYMOND WILLIAMS

Dylan Thomas
KARL SHAPIRO

C. B. Cox, the editor of this volume in
the Twentieth Century Views series, is
Senior Lecturer in English at the University of Hull, England, and was Visiting Associate Professor at the University
of California at Berkeley during 1964-65.
Co-editor of *The Critical Quarterly,* he
is also the author of *The Free Spirit,* a
study of the development of the modern
novel, and co-author of *Modern Poetry*
and *Practical Criticism,* among other
works.

TWENTIETH CENTURY VIEWS

The aim of this series is to present the best in contemporary critical opinion on major authors, providing a twentieth century perspective on their changing status in an era of profound revaluation.

Maynard Mack, *Series Editor*
Yale University

DYLAN THOMAS

A COLLECTION OF CRITICAL ESSAYS

Edited by

C. B. Cox

Prentice-Hall, Inc., *Englewood Cliffs, N.J.*

A SPECTRUM BOOK

The author wishes to thank J. M. Dent & Sons Ltd.,
the Trustees of the Dylan Thomas Estate, and New
Directions Publishing Corporation for permission to
use material from *The Collected Poems of Dylan Thomas*,
copyright © 1953 by Dylan Thomas, copyright © 1957
by New Directions Publishing Corporation

Current printing (last number):

10 9 8 7 6 5 4 3 2 1

Contents

Introduction

by C. B. Cox

"Drunk with melody, and what the words were he cared not." [1]
This view, pronounced by Robert Graves in his 1954-55 Clark lectures at Cambridge, was common among early commentators on Dylan Thomas. During his lecture Graves offered a £1 note to anyone who could make sense of the opening lines of Thomas's poem " 'If my head hurt a hair's foot.' " When M. J. C. Hodgart came forward to claim the money, offering the now well-known interpretation that the unborn child in the womb is addressing the mother, Graves remained unconvinced.

If Graves made such an offer today, he could expect a queue of students demanding payment. They would have only to look up the poem in William York Tindall's useful *A Reader's Guide to Dylan Thomas* (1962), where it is explained that "nothing by Thomas could be plainer than this debate between embryo and mother." [2] In his introduction Tindall even goes so far as to assert that "close reading and comparison of texts prove Thomas as rational and orderly as any poet this side of Alexander Pope." [3]

Tindall's book demonstrates the considerable change in critical opinion that has taken place in the last decade. Thomas's early admirers could not understand his poems, but found in him an inspired bard; his music and rhetoric moved them to apocalyptic visions. Edith Sitwell proclaimed: "His voice resembles no other voice; the spirit is that of the beginning of created things: there is here no case of a separate imagination, of invention. From the

[1] Robert Graves, *The Crowning Privilege* (London: Cassell and Co., Ltd., 1955), p. 132.
[2] William York Tindall, *A Reader's Guide to Dylan Thomas* (New York: Farrar, Straus and Co., Inc., 1962), p. 173.
[3] *Ibid.*, p. 11.

depths of Being, from the roots of the world, a voice speaks." [4]
Thomas's hostile critics, such as Geoffrey Grigson in his article "How
Much Me Now Your Acrobatics Amaze" or the reviewers in the English magazine *Scrutiny*, found it easy to combat such enthusiasm by
charging him with incoherence. For Grigson, Thomas's poems
"sprawl loosely, below the waist" and "his words come up bubbling
in an automatic muddle." [5]

Such praise and condemnation now appear to some extent misin-
formed. Particularly since the publication in 1957 of Thomas's letters to Vernon Watkins it has been realized that he not only was an
artful maker of complicated rhythms and verse structures, but also
cared very much what the words meant. His discussions with Watkins show that he knew precisely what effects he intended, and to
some degree justify his controversial claim that his poems should be
read "literally." The notebooks in the Lockwood Memorial Library
of the State University of New York at Buffalo prove how carefully
he revised; and a number of recent theses have helped to clear up
many of the obscure points in his work. Typical of the best of this
kind of scholarship is H. H. Kleinman's *The Religious Sonnets of
Dylan Thomas* (1963), which includes detailed study of the background material from which Thomas drew his imagery. A new
Thomas has emerged, very different from the ranting, inspired
Welshman of many early portraits.

This new understanding of Thomas does not mean, however, that
controversy is ended. Academic scholars may too easily believe that
their growing insight into his meaning necessarily leads to a higher
estimate of his poetry. After his death in 1953 a reaction to his influence began, and many young poets of the 1950s, particularly in
England, felt his experiments in syntax and imagery were pretentious. In his introduction to the "Movement" anthology *New Lines*
(1956), Robert Conquest clearly had Thomas in mind when he la-
mented that in the 1940s poets "were encouraged to regard their
task simply as one of making an arrangement of images of sex and
violence tapped straight from the unconscious (a sort of upper-mid-
dle-brow equivalent of the horror-comic), or to evoke without com-

[4] Edith Sitwell, *The Atlantic Book of British and American Poetry* (Boston:
Atlantic-Little, Brown and Co., 1958), p. 982.
[5] Geoffrey Grigson, *The Harp of Aeolus* (London: Routledge and Kegan Paul,
Ltd., 1948), pp. 154, 156.

ment the *naïvetés* and nostalgias of childhood." [6] The poets included in his anthology no longer sought a new language to represent the warring elements in their unconscious, or the chaos of modern society; they returned instead to traditional "rational" forms of communication. They saw themselves not as inspired bards, but as men speaking to men—a reaction to Thomas which was also part of a larger revolt against the critical theories of T. S. Eliot and post-symbolist art. In his brilliant book *Articulate Energy* (1955), Donald Davie accused Thomas of indulging in "pseudo-syntax," abandoning the task of articulation so that the objects to which he refers, tumbled pell-mell together, can no longer be identified.[7] Unfortunately Davie's comments on Thomas are so brief, and so closely tied to his general argument, that they cannot fairly be included in this anthology. Davie placed Thomas among those modern poets who fail because their work falls into isolated units. The sentences that seem to drive forward in time through their verbs do no such thing, for the poems proceed by repetition rather than by the establishment of proper syntactical arrangements between beginning, middle, and end. For Davie, the abandonment of syntax testified to a failure of the poet's nerve, "a loss of confidence in the intelligible structure of the conscious mind, and the validity of its activity." [8]

Our attitude to Davie's criticism must depend, to a large extent, on how far we sympathize with the view that Thomas could only express the confusion in which we live by a complete break with orthodox forms of articulation. At a first reading the surface brilliance of the early poems suggests a violent, uncontrollable energy; but, as Robert M. Adams asks in his essay on Crashaw and Thomas: "Is it a defensible aesthetic position to say that so long as each individual section of his poem is built on sufficiently violent and intensive contrasts the poet need provide no structure of mood, tone, imagery, temporal order, or grammatical assertion?" Justifications of Thomas's technical innovations often refer to his famous letter to Henry Treece, in which he argues that his poems develop through a series of contradictory images.[9] This theory, as John Bayley points out,

---

[6] Robert Conquest, ed., *New Lines* (London: Macmillan and Co., Ltd., 1956), p. xiv.

[7] Donald Davie, *Articulate Energy* (London: Routledge and Kegan Paul, Ltd., 1955), pp. 125-27.

[8] *Ibid.*, p. 129.

[9] The passage is quoted by John Bayley on page 154.

sounds more impressive than it is, but it does reveal Thomas's obsession with the inter-involvement of creation and destruction, life and death. In poem after poem he questions the meaning of his own genesis. Particularly in the early poetry, this conflict is presented through puns such as "worm" or "seedy," through dialogue poems such as "I see the boys of summer," and through a repeated "war" between opposite kinds of imagery. The theme is not developed logically, for progress in the poem is achieved through verbal play, repetition, and incantation. Whether in these poems Thomas achieves "rational" control, as Tindall suggests, is still a very open question. In the excerpt from his *The Romantic Survival* included in this anthology, John Bayley examines this method of composition with great care, and his final judgments are among the most definitive yet published.

This leads to a further critical problem. In his late poems such as "Poem in October," "Fern Hill," and "Over Sir John's hill," Thomas achieved a new lucidity and serenity, and many readers have felt that in the 1940s he at last began to solve his technical problems; yet William Empson, in a review reprinted in this anthology, admits that he prefers the early obscure poems. Is it true that in the early poems Thomas discovered a form which communicated fully the strain under which he lived, and that the later poems withdraw from such problems into nostalgia? Or do the later poems emerge from womb and tomb into light?

Another recent English writer, David Holbrook, has criticized the subconscious psychological motives underlying Thomas's obscurity. There is evidence that as he revised his poems their obscurity increased. It is also true that for twenty years he proved incomprehensible to some of the most perceptive critics and poets of his time (even Tindall, with all his perspicacity, has to admit that the meaning of some poems still escapes him) and that most of the spellbound listeners to his inspired readings had little idea what the poems were about. In his book *Dylan Thomas and Poetic Dissociation* (1964),[10] Holbrook argues that Thomas developed his imagery of wombs and tombs, sex and corpses, as a means of protecting himself against adult reality. In spite of Thomas's care in preparing his work, his poems effect a kind of "hallucination" or "dissociated phantasy." He invented "a babble-language which concealed the nature of real-

[10] Published in England as *Llareggub Revisited: Dylan Thomas and the State of Modern Poetry.*

ity from himself and his readers—and in its very oral sensationalism, in its very meaninglessness, it represented for him and his readers a satisfying return to the delusions of that stage of infancy when we tend to resist the uncomfortable exigencies and losses consequent upon the development of a growing reality sense. This may be linked with the man's alcoholism and his sexual promiscuity." [11]

There is clearly some evidence for Holbrook's argument that Thomas could never accept an adult sexual relationship. His Welsh Protestant conscience appears to have been disgusted and shocked by his first experiences with women, and all his life he felt driven by uncontrollable sexual impulses. The famous pranks and the hard drinking also suggest some kind of neurotic alienation from ordinary life. Holbrook goes too far, however, when he accuses Thomas of inventing a "babble-language" to cover up his own psychological problems. Thomas had acquired a popular knowledge of Freud and Jung, and it can be argued that his understanding of the irrational power sex holds over human life is decidedly realistic. Among a list of poems he finds meaningless Holbrook includes "Love in the Asylum." In this poem the image of the madhouse is used to depict how sex invades the mind:

> A stranger has come
> To share my room in the house not right in the head,
> A girl mad as birds . . . [12]

The images in the poem deliberately represent the confusions brought by sex, the sense of delusion, the jealousy and suffering, and the possibility of vision. The double meaning of the title, with love as refuge and madhouse, sums up the conflict in Thomas's attitudes to sex. Into his own personal nightmares, the madhouse of his ordinary life, intrudes sex, equally irrational and demented; yet in the arms of the woman he may escape into "the first vision that set fire to the stars."

In the 1930s Thomas read the surrealist magazine, *transition,* and in 1936 he visited the International Surrealist Exhibition in the New Burlington Galleries at London. The many references to dreams and madness in both his poetry and prose reflect this interest in irrational forms of art. The wild fantasies of Gothic romance

[11] David Holbrook, *Dylan Thomas and Poetic Dissociation* (Carbondale: Southern Illinois University Press, 1964), p. 78.

[12] *The Collected Poems of Dylan Thomas.* (New York: New Directions, 1957), p. 119.

provided nineteenth century romantics with a means of representing violent emotions unacknowledged by the conventions of their society; so the ghosts, vampires, and witches of Thomas's poems depict the nightmare powers in control of man. These alien forces are most often associated with sex, but there are also a number of poems where he reacts with horror to the madness of war. He was born in October 1914, at the very time when the young men of Europe were about to die by the millions on the Western Front:

> I dreamed my genesis and died again, shrapnel
> Rammed in the marching heart, hole
> In the stitched wound and clotted wind, muzzled
> Death on the mouth that ate the gas.[13]

His own birth thus represented for Thomas that mingling of creative and destructive forces in nature which is his perpetual theme. Appalled by the suffering and killing in the two wars, he found it difficult to impose any rational sense on this horror. His imagination found a more appropriate expression in opposing and contradictory images.

In his writings, however, Thomas resisted the attractions of surrealism and struggled against complete submission to the anarchic and the irrational. In prose and poetry alike he sought self-understanding, and his work accordingly offers repeated portraits of the artist. By exhortation, bardic gestures, and assertive rhythms, he labours to coerce his readers and himself into acceptance of life. By exuberant fancies, wit, and gaiety, he exorcises the powers of darkness, or at least contains them within a bound they dare not pass. As the careful arrangement of stanza and rhyme conflicts with the neurotic reaction to sex in "Love in the Asylum," so throughout his poetry verbal play and exhilaration of language work against images of sterility and disgust. Of his poem "A Refusal to Mourn the Death, by Fire, of a Child in London" Empson writes that "the poet says he will not say what he says." [14] His refusal to mourn is a form of mourning; so in many poems, such as "And death shall have no dominion" and "Do not go gentle into that good night," the assertions ask for the impossible. At times the rhetoric moves close to hysteria, but Thomas is determined to create, to build his ark on the flood of life. Although harried by personal nightmares, he seeks for some

[13] *Ibid.*, p. 33.
[14] Quoted in Tindall, *Reader's Guide*, p. 181.

means of self-control, and for some life to celebrate. Karl Shapiro
finds in Thomas evidence of a split mind, mixing sexual revulsion
and sexual ecstasy, puritanism and mysticism, the pathological and
the joyous. John Bayley offers a final justification for this conflict
in Thomas's work:

> At a time when the language of poetry has seemed to be in danger of
> being pulled apart between the meaningless exuberance of surrealism
> on the one hand, and the self-conscious precision of poets influenced
> by positivistic theory on the other, he has achieved a balance between
> the two, in his best poems, while retaining—and even drawing our
> attention to—the separateness of both.

II

My anthology begins with a lively review of *Collected Poems* written by John Wain in 1953 for a small magazine. This is followed by
another useful introductory essay, in which David Daiches pays trib-
ute to Thomas's courageous celebration of life. John Ackerman's
essay provides the most recent analysis of the Welsh influence on
Thomas. In an excellent review of Ackerman's book, John Wain
pointed out that the hostile English critics of Thomas are often ob-
jecting to his Welshness, "the open emotionalism, the large verbal
gestures which seem to them mere rant, the rapt pleasure in elaborate craftsmanship, and above all the bardic tone." [15] The question
of Welsh influence had previously been examined in a valuable article by Geoffrey Moore.[16] Ackerman discusses in detail the concept of
the bard in Wales, the influence of Nonconformity, and Thomas's
relation to other Anglo-Welsh writers.

Elder Olson's *The Poetry of Dylan Thomas* was the first full-
length study of Thomas's language. Recent scholars such as Kleinman have extended and modified Olson's insights, but his first
chapter, which I have printed here, asks the fundamental questions.
Olson is particularly stimulating in his analysis of the enormous
power and strangeness of Thomas's imagination. Olson's book has
been followed, in the *Explicator* and other journals, by a spate of
detailed analyses of poems. Winifred Nowottny's interpretation of

[15] John Wain. "Dylan Thomas Today," *The New York Review of Books*, IV
(Feb. 25, 1965), p. 14.
[16] Geoffrey Moore, "Dylan Thomas," in E. W. Tedlock, ed., *Dylan Thomas:
The Legend and the Poet*. (London: William Heinemann, 1960), pp. 248-268.

"There was a Saviour," from her valuable book *The Language Poets Use,* is particularly thorough and searching; she examines in detail "all the directives for interpretation that the poet has built into his poem," [17] and concludes that this kind of richly meaningful verse enables the English language itself to expand. This is followed by Ralph Maud's excellent analysis of "Over Sir John's hill." Ralph Maud has established himself as one of the leading Thomas scholars, and this chapter from his book *Entrances to Dylan Thomas' Poetry* demonstrates the value of viewing the published poems in the perspective of a detailed knowledge of Thomas's manuscripts. William Empson's famous *New Statesman* review of *Collected Poems* and *Under Milk Wood* is followed by two opposing views of *Under Milk Wood,* one by Raymond Williams and the other by David Holbrook, both taking account of the influence of James Joyce, but coming to very different conclusions on the merit of the work. Annis Pratt contributes an essay, specially adapted for *Twentieth Century Views,* which deals with the whole body of Thomas's prose. Continuing the explorations by those who have discerned significant parallels between Thomas and seventeenth century metaphysical poets, Robert M. Adams compares Thomas to Crashaw, and asks fundamental questions about our current taste for the incongruous and the grotesque. John Bayley provides a masterly summing up of the technical problems in Thomas's work, and Karl Shapiro's brilliant comprehensive estimate of Thomas's achievement brings the volume to a close.

Although recent criticism of Thomas is full of new explanations and insights, his poetry remains confusing, disturbing, never completely explicable. For example, many commentators have found the line "Light breaks where no sun shines" memorable, but have been defeated when they tried to explain why. Thomas offers a dream landscape, devoid of life, devoid of the fertility brought by the sun, like that of a strange planet in a science fiction story. Here light breaks; in all this bleakness, typical of modern experience, some clarity may yet be possible. The image holds its contradictions and refuses to resolve them. The explanations are inadequate; so it may well be that when we, his twentieth century critics, are forgotten, Thomas's poetry will continue to stimulate controversy, and to give pleasure "for as long as forever is."

[17] Winifred Nowottny, *The Language Poets Use* (London: The Athlone Press, 1962), p. 220.

Dylan Thomas:
A Review of His Collected Poems

by John Wain

Reviewing this volume[1] is not, in the ordinary sense, reviewing at all. Here are the poems we have all been familiar with for years, which have been explored, acclaimed, damned, rejected, and worshipped throughout the entire adult life of anyone aged less than thirty-five; and "reviewing" them is merely a matter of passing them round and giving each critic an opportunity to say where he, personally, stands with regard to Mr. Thomas's work.

Most people have said their say by now; this would be, if one could be bothered, a good opportunity to survey the kind of thing that had been said. But I doubt if any such summary could, at this stage, be useful or entertaining: most kinds of critical mistakes have been made in dealing with these poems, and will no doubt go on being made, and that is about all there is to it. The wild overpraise of Thomas's original backers was answered by the savage onslaught of those who felt that the whole thing had gone too far, and by about 1946 one felt that the critics were quite simply talking to each other rather than the public, and certainly not bothering overmuch about the poems. The small-arms fire has now grown so hot that anyone who shows his head is sure to be riddled from some quarter. For instance, Mr. Read's famous "these poems cannot be reviewed: they can only be acclaimed" (*of Twenty-Five Poems*) drew such furious abuse and raillery that nowadays no one dare be so outspoken, even if they feel really strongly impelled to praise Thomas;

[1] Dylan Thomas, *Collected Poems*, 1934-52.

9

and so one finds, for instance, a Sunday reviewer saying that "it need no longer be eccentric" to say that Thomas is the greatest living writer of English poetry. What he meant was that he thought so himself, but did not dare say so outright in case some anti-Thomas bully came round to thrash him, so had to dress it up with a meaningless qualification. In that particular case, of course, it is unnecessary to do more than say No; it is, clearly, eccentric, not to say imperceptive, to call Thomas the greatest living writer of English verse so long as Eliot is still writing, to say nothing of Auden, Graves, and several others. At the other extreme we have the disgraceful treatment of Thomas in *Scrutiny,* which is, I am afraid, only typical of that magazine's bad record over contemporary poetry in general. It is rather significant that the best review of this collection should have appeared in the *New Statesman*—a paper for whose criticism *Scrutiny* can never say a good word.

But I must get on with the job, which is to say briefly (for what it is worth) where I stand on the Thomas question. I think, then, that he is a fine, bold, original, and strong poet whose work is marred by two great drawbacks. First, a disastrously limited subject-matter. There are really only three subjects treated: (i) childhood, and the associated topic of what it is like to remember one's childhood; (ii) the viscera; (iii) religion. The first is very well handled, but really nobody could improve on the *Portrait of the Artist as a Young Dog* as saying all that can be said about growing up, and if you add the related group of verse pieces, chiefly the quasi-Wordsworthian "Poem in October," you really find that there is nothing left to do. The second, the viscera, is of course an important subject, and the early poems with their obsessive concern with anatomy and crude physical sensation are fine and valuable poems; but here again you can say the last word, and say it pretty quickly. Thomas has added almost no good love poetry to the language, because he always seems to treat sexual love as an affair of glandular secretions and the mingling of fluids, which is only true as far as it goes. The third subject, religion, seems to me Thomas's worst pitch; he never succeeds in making me feel that he is doing more than thumbing a lift from it. Indeed it is only a helpful subject to him in those poems which are content to leave every important matter to be settled by the reader: the line "After the first death, there is no other" has been praised as an example of significant ambiguity (either "when you are dead there's an end of it" or "after this mortal life comes the eternal one"), and no doubt that is very valuable, but if a poet is going to be a religious poet there has (one would think) to be a little more definition about it.

This leads on to the second great flaw which keeps Thomas's poetry at a remove from greatness: the suspicion (which has, goodness knows, been voiced often enough) that his writing, in the more "difficult" poems, is quasi-automatic. It is perfectly possible to furnish even his wildest pieces with a "meaning" (*i.e.*, a paraphrasable content or set of alternative paraphrasable contents), but the gnawing doubt remains as to whether the writer really *cared* whether it meant anything precise or not. This, of course, is the great point that has to be settled; not until every one of the more obscure poems has been thoroughly thrashed out (as, in time, they will be) can we feel confident of reaching an answer. Meanwhile we want a little less gas about Thomas, and some criticism that really talks turkey and gets down to particular instances. The thing is, meanwhile, very worrying to the honest reader. Take, for instance, the line

And I am struck as lonely as a holy maker by the sun.

Why does the sun strike a holy maker lonely? Or rather, to put first things first, does it just strike the poet lonely, as lonely as a holy maker? Of course a holy maker is lonely, whether the expression means (i) a specifically religious poet, (ii) just any poet ("all makers are holy"), (iii) God. This third suggestion comes from a friend who said it was "obvious" that the line referred to God creating the sun, and feeling lonely because for the first time there existed in the universe something with which it was possible to have a relationship, and therefore the concept of loneliness appeared. But if so, why "a" holy maker and not "the"? At this point, does one plunge ahead, hoping to reach the further shore, or does one simply go back in despair and say that the effect is of a latter-day Swinburne, who just wants to make a nice noise? Answers to these and all the other questions of interpretation are easy to supply; but (and this is the point) they are not easy to cleanse, when supplied, of a certain *voulu* or factitious quality.

This, by the way, would be the place for a few remarks in contradiction of one of the most obstinate absurdities that bedevil discussion of this poet: the idea, brought up on occasion by his supporters and opponents alike, that he is a divinely inspired simpleton; what Mr. Eliot, speaking of Blake, called "a wild pet for the super-cultivated." His association in the public mind with Miss Sitwell, who is simply not interested in the ordinary processes of being intelligent, has helped to put this nonsense about, but it is obvious to anyone who reads the poems carefully that Thomas puts into them a good deal of ordinary common-or-garden cleverness and capability of the breadwinning, examination-passing type, not a fanciful fourth-dimensional "poetic" afflatus. This is clear from the very great skill with which he has assimilated his literary influences, the chief of which are, of course, Hopkins and Yeats, though there is a noticeable streak of William Empson (cleverly combined with the Yeats influence in one of the new poems here, the villanelle). Thomas is also a brilliant parodist, another sure test of acuteness of the ordinary day-to-day type (no fool ever wrote a successful parody even if, which I doubt, a fool ever wrote a successful poem).

To turn definitely to the credit side, there is, of course, all the obvious—magnificently and overwhelmingly obvious—grandeur, generosity, and harmony of these poems. The superb balance of rhymes in "The Conversation of Prayer," for instance, is something to be grateful for; doubly so when one thinks that Thomas came of literary age at a time when the typical successful poet was getting away with lines like these:

> You who go out alone, on tandem or on pillion,
> Down arterial roads riding in April,
> Or sad beside lakes where hill-slopes are reflected
> Making fires of leaves, your high hopes fallen:
> Cyclists and hikers in company, day excursionists,
> Refugees from cursed towns and devastated areas;
> Know you seek a new world, a saviour to establish
> Long-lost kinship and restore the blood's fulfilment.

Compare:

> Once it was the colour of saying
> Soaked my table the uglier side of a hill
> With a capsized field where a school sat still
> And a black and white patch of girls grew playing;
> The gentle seaslides of saying I must undo
> That all the charmingly drowned arise to cockcrow and kill.

If the Thomas passage shows the tendency towards over-richness and artfulness (the field is "capsized" because there is a school sitting still in it, and schoolboys wear caps, as well as because it is tilted on the side of a hill), one forgives it at once by comparison with the utter nullity of the other extract, which incidentally I chose from an anthology and did not ferret out from among the author's early and buried work. In the criticism of contemporary literature, one's standards are bound to be, essentially, comparative; we cannot know what will interest posterity, but that Thomas's poems will continue to interest the men of his own time cannot be questioned and need not, certainly, be grudged.

The Poetry of Dylan Thomas

by David Daiches

The sudden and premature death of Dylan Thomas produced elegies and appreciations in extraordinary numbers on both sides of the Atlantic. Thomas was the most poetical poet of our time. He talked and dressed and behaved and lived like a poet; he was reckless, flamboyant, irreverent, innocent, bawdy and bibulous. His verse, too, had a romantic wildness about it that even a reader who could make nothing of it recognized as "poetic." In the February 1954 issue of the *London Magazine* a twenty-six-year-old poet wrote a letter saying that Thomas represented the "archetypal picture of the Poet" for his generation, and that the death of this wild and generous character produced "something like a panic" in the world of letters. He was answered in the next issue of the magazine by a thirty-one-year-old poet who said that this was puerile nonsense and deplored what he called the "fulsome ballyhoo" which Thomas's death evoked in both England and America. There was perhaps an element of ballyhoo in the spate of articles about Thomas, but sober critical judgment is difficult when one is writing of a brilliant young man who has died at the very height of his career (or at the very height of his promise; we shall never tell now). And surely the exaggeration of the sense of loss at the death of a poet is a sign of health in any culture? Now that the shock has worn off, however, we can turn more soberly to ask the question: What sort of poetry did Dylan Thomas write, and how good is it?

In a note to the collected edition of his poems, Thomas wrote: "These poems, with all their crudities, doubts, and confusions, are written for the love of Man and in praise of God. . . ." And in his prologue to the same volume he proclaimed his intention of celebrating the world and all that is in it:

> . . . as I hack
> This rumpus of shapes
> For you to know
> How I, a spinning man,
> Glory also this star, bird
> Roared, sea born, man torn, blood blest.
> Hark: I trumpet the place,
> From fish to jumping hill! Look:
> I build my bellowing ark
> To the best of my love
> As the flood begins,
> Out of the fountainhead
> Of fear, rage red, manalive, . . .

This prologue is a great hail to the natural world, and man as a part of it, and might be taken by the careless reader as an impressionist outpouring of celebratory exclamations:

> Huloo, my prowed dove with a flute!
> Ahoy, old, sea-legged fox,
> Tom tit and Dai mouse!
> My ark sings in the sun
> At God speeded summer's end
> And the flood flowers now.

Yet in fact this spontaneous-seeming poem is a cunningly contrived work in two movements of fifty-one lines each, with the second section rhyming backwards with the first—the first line rhyming with the last, the second with the second last, and so on, the only pair of adjacent lines which rhyme being the fifty-first and the fifty-second. Whether the ear catches this complicated cross rhyming or not, it is part of a cunning pattern of ebb and flow, of movement and countermovement, which runs through the poem. This single piece of evidence is perhaps enough to prove that, for all the appearance of spontaneity and sometimes of free association that his poems present to some readers, Thomas was a remarkably conscientious craftsman for whom meaning was bound up with pattern and order. No modern poet in English has had a keener sense of form or has handled stanzas and verse paragraphs—whether traditional or original—with more deliberate cunning.

It is worth stressing this at the outset because there are still some people who talk of Thomas as though he were a writer of an inspired mad rhetoric, of glorious, tumbling, swirling language which fell from his pen in magnificent disorder. He has been held up by some as the antithesis of Eliot and his school, renouncing the cerebral orderliness of the 1920s and the 1930s in favour of a new romanticism, an engaging irresponsibility. On the other hand there are those who discuss his poems as though they are merely texts for exposition, ignoring the rhyme scheme and the complicated verbal and visual patterning to concentrate solely on the intellectual implications of the images. The truth is that Thomas is neither a whirling romantic nor a metaphysical imagist, but a poet who uses pattern and metaphor in a complex craftsmanship in order to create a ritual of celebration. He sees life as a continuous process, sees the workings of biology as a magical transformation producing unity out of identity, identity out of unity, the generations linked with one another and man linked with nature. Again and again in his early poems he seeks to find a poetic ritual for the celebration of this identity:

> Before I knocked and flesh let enter,
> With liquid hands tapped on the womb,
> I who was shapeless as the water
> That shaped the Jordan near my home
> Was brother to Mnetha's daughter
> And sister to the fathering worm.

Or again:

> The force that through the green fuse drives the flower
> Drives my green age; that blasts the roots of trees
> Is my destroyer.

And most clearly of all:

> This bread I break was once the oat,
> This wine upon a foreign tree
> Plunged in its fruit;
> Man in the day or wind at night
> Laid the crops low, broke the grape's joy . . .
>
> This flesh you break, this blood you let
> Make desolation in the vein,
> Were oat and grape
> Born of the sensual root and sap;
> My wine you drink, my bread you snap.

Man is locked in a round of identities; the beginning of growth is also the first movement towards death, the beginning of love is the first move towards procreation, which in turn moves towards new growth, and the only way out of time's squirrel-cage is to embrace the unity of man with nature, of the generations with each other, of the divine with the human, of life with death, to see the glory and the wonder of it. If we ignore the cosmic round to seize the moment when we think we have it, we are both deluded and doomed:

> I see the boys of summer in their ruin
> Lay the gold tithings barren,
> Setting no store by harvest, freeze the soils;
> There in their heat the winter floods
> Of frozen loves they fetch their girls,
> And drown the cargoed apples in their tides.
>
> Those boys of light are curdlers in their folly,
> Sour the boiling honey; . . .

This is from an early poem; and several of these early poems strike this note—the note of doom in the midst of present pleasure, for concealed in each moment lie change and death. Thomas did not rush towards the celebration of unity in all life and all time which later became an important theme of comfort for him; he moved to it through disillusion and experiment. The force that drives the flower and the tree to full burgeoning and then to death would destroy him also. Only later came the realization that such destruction is no destruction, but a guarantee of immortality, of perpetual life in a cosmic eternity:

> And death shall have no dominion.
> Dead men naked they shall be one
> With the man in the wind and the west moon;
> When their bones are picked clean and the clean bones gone,
> They shall have stars at elbow and foot;
> Though they go mad they shall be sane,
> Though they sink through the sea they shall rise again;
> Though lovers be lost love shall not;
> And death shall have no dominion.

It is this thought that sounds the note of triumph in "Ceremony After a Fire Raid" and which provides the comfort in "A Refusal to Mourn the Death, by Fire, of a Child in London."

"A Refusal to Mourn" is a poem worth pausing at, for it illus-
trates not only a characteristic theme of what might be called the
middle Thomas, but also a characteristic way of handling the theme.
The poem is ritualistic in tone; its dominant images are sacramental; and the cunningly contrived rise and fall of the cadence of each
stanza adds to the note of formal ceremony. There are four stanzas,
the first two and one line of the third containing a single sentence
which swells out to a magnificent surge of meaning. Then, after a
pause, the final stanza makes a concluding ritual statement, an an-
tiphonal chant answering the first three stanzas. The paraphrasable
meaning of the poem is simple enough: the poet is saying that never,
until the end of the world and the final return of all things to their
primal elements, will he distort the meaning of the child's death by
mourning. One dies but once, and through that death becomes re-
united with the timeless unity of things. But the paraphrasable
meaning is not, of course, the meaning of the poem, which is expanded at each point through a deliberately sacramental imagery
while at the same time the emotion is controlled and organized by
the cadences of the stanza. The first stanza and a half describe the
end of the world as a return from differentiated identity to elemental unity:

> Never until the mankind making   *Middle*
> Bird beast and flower
> Fathering and all humbling darkness
> Tells with silence the last light breaking
> And the still hour
> Is come of the sea tumbling in harness
>
> And I must enter again the round
> Zion of the water bead
> And the synagogue of the ear of corn
> Shall I let pray the shadow of a sound
> Or sow my salt seed
> In the least valley of sackcloth to mourn
>
> The majesty and burning of the child's death . . .

There is no obscurity here, to anybody who knows Thomas's idiom.
We have only to recall "This bread I break was once the oat" to
realize the significance of the first three lines of the second stanza.
The water bead and the ear of corn are symbolic primal elements,

to which all return at the end. But why "*Zion* of the water bead" and "*synagogue* of the ear of corn"? The answer is simply that these are sacramental images intended to give a sacramental meaning to the statement. It is a kind of imagery of which Thomas is very fond (one can find numerous other examples, among them such a phrase as "the parables of sun light" in "Poem in October" or his use of Adam and Christ in his earlier poems). One might still ask why he says "synagogue" and not "church." The answer, I think, is that he wants to shock the reader into attention to the sacramental meaning. A more everyday religious word might pass by as a conventional poetic image, but "synagogue" attracts our attention at once; it has no meaning other than its literal one, and therefore can be used freshly in a non-literal way. The third stanza continues:

> I shall not murder
> The mankind of her going with a grave truth
> Nor blaspheme down the stations of the breath
> With any further
> Elegy of innocence and youth.

Here words like "mankind," "blaspheme," "stations of the breath" (recalling "stations of the Cross") play an easily discernible part in the expansion of the meaning, while the pun in "grave truth" represents a device common enough in modern poetry. The concluding stanza gives the reason, the counter-statement:

> Deep with the first dead lies London's daughter,
> Robed in the long friends,
> The grains beyond age, the dark veins of her mother,
> Secret by the unmourning water
> Of the riding Thames.
> After the first death, there is no other.

This echoes, in its own way, the opening stanza; but its tone is new; it is that of liturgical proclamation. We need not wince at the suggestion that "long friends" means (among other things) worms; worms for Thomas were not disgusting, but profoundly symbolic: like maggots they are elements of corruption and thus of reunification, of eternity.

How much a poem of this kind owes to the imagery and to the cadence, as well as to the careful patterning, can be seen at once if

one takes the perhaps extreme method of turning its paraphrasable
content into conventional rhymed verse:

> Not until doomsday's final call
> And all the earth returns once more
> To that primaeval home of all,
> When on that insubstantial shore
> The tumbling primal waters foam
> And silence rules her lonely home,
>
> And I return to whence I came,
> The sacramental child of earth,
> Joining with nature to proclaim
> A death that is a second birth—
> No, not until that final sleep
> Will I for this dead infant weep.
>
> She lies with her ancestral dead,
> The child of London, home at last
> To earth from whence all life is bred
> And present mingles with the past.
> The unmourning waters lap her feet:
> She has no second death to meet.

This is doggerel, of course, but it contains, in however crude a form,
the essential paraphrasable meaning of the Thomas poem—yet
misses everything of any significance about it. The note of ritual, of
sacrament, of celebration, achieved through his special use of imagery and by other devices, is central in Thomas's poetry.

I have not given a critical analysis of the poem, but merely suggested a way of looking at it. "A Refusal to Mourn" is a characteristic poem of one phase of Thomas's career, during which he was
drawing together his impressions of the unity of all creation and all
time to serve the purpose of a specific occasion. His earlier poems
often fail by being too packed with metaphor suggestive of identity.
Words like "Adam," "Christ," "ghost," "worm," "womb," phrases
like "the mouth of time," "death's feather," "beach of flesh," "hatch-
ing hair," "half-tracked thigh" abound, and though each has its
orderly place in the poem the reader often feels dulled by the continuous impact of repeated words of this kind. The sonnet-sequence,
"Altar-wise by owl-light," contains some brilliant identifying imagery (suggesting the identity of man with Christ, of creation with

death, of history with the present), but it is altogether too closely packed, too dense, to come across effectively. The opening is almost a self-parody:

> Altarwise by owl-light in the half-way house
> The gentleman lay graveward with his furies;
> Abaddon in the hangnail cracked from Adam,
> And, from his fork, a dog among the fairies,
> The atlas-eater with a jaw for news,
> Bit out the mandrake with to-morrow's scream. . . .

The careful explicator will be able to produce informative glosses on each of these phrases, but the fact remains that the poem is congested with its metaphors, and the reader is left with a feeling of oppression. A fair number of Thomas's earlier poems are obscure for this reason. It is not the obscurity of free association or of references to private reading, but an obscurity which results from an attempt to pack too much into a short space, to make every comma tell, as it were. With his continuous emphasis on birth, prenatal life, the relation of parent to child, growth, the relation of body and spirit, of life to death, of human and animal to vegetable, and similar themes, and his constant search for devices to celebrate these and identify them with each other, he does not want one word to slip which may help in building up the total pattern of meaning. One of his poems shows how the making of continuous connections and identities can bewilder the reader:

> Today, this insect, and the world I breathe,
> Now that my symbols have outelbowed space,
> Time at the city spectacles, and half
> The dear, daft time I take to nudge the sentence,
> In trust and tale have I divided sense,
> Slapped down the guillotine, the blood-red double
> Of head and tail made witnesses to this
> Murder of Eden and green genesis.

He is saying here, in his compact metaphorical way, that expression in language (which means expression in time) breaks up and so distorts the original vision. In his desire to avoid that breaking up he sometimes piles up the images and metaphors until the reader simply cannot construe the lines (as in the sixth stanza of "When, like a running grave"). But it must be emphasized that this is not the fault of a bad romantic poetry, too loose and exclamatory, but comes from what can perhaps be called the classical vice of attempting to press too much into a little space.

Thomas progressed from those poems in which his techniques of identification are sometimes pressed too far, through a period of "occasional" verse in which he focussed his general notions on particular incidents and situations to give a grave and formal ceremonial poetry ("A Refusal to Mourn," "Do not go gentle into that good night." "On the Marriage of a Virgin," etc.) to a period of more limpid, open-worked poetry in which, instead of endeavouring to leap outside time into a pantheistic cosmos beyond the dimensions, he accepts time and change and uses memory as an elegiac device ("Poem in October," "Fern Hill," "Over Sir John's hill," "Poem on his birthday"). But these divisions are not strictly chronological, nor do they take account of all the kinds of verse he was writing. There is, for example, "A Winter's Tale," a "middle" poem, which handles a universal folk theme with a quiet beauty that results from perfect control of the imagery. It is far too long a poem to quote, and it needs to be read as a whole to be appreciated; it is one of Thomas's half dozen truly magnificent poems.

Another remarkable poem which does not quite fit into my threefold classification is "Vision and Prayer," a finely wrought pattern-poem in two parts of six stanzas each. In no other poem has Thomas so successfully handled the theme of the identity of himself, everyman, and Christ. He imagines himself addressing the unborn Christ, who, in his mother's womb, seems separated from himself by a "wall thin as a wren's bone." The infant in the next room replies, explaining that it is his destiny to storm out across the partition that separates man from God, and the poet identifies himself with the glory and suffering of Christ's redemptive career. The first part of the poem blazes to a conclusion with a vision of the triumph and pain of Christ's death. The second movement begins in a slow, hushed, almost muttering cadence: the poet prays that Christ remain in the womb, for men are indifferent and wanton and not worth redemption. Let the splendour of Christ's martyrdom remain unrevealed; "May the crimson/ Sun spin a grave grey/ And the colour of clay/ Stream upon his martyrdom." But as he ends this sad prayer the sun of God blazes forth and takes up the poet in its lightning. "The sun roars at the prayer's end." No summary or partial quotation can do justice to the force and brilliance of this most cunningly modulated poem. The stanzas of the first part are diamond-shaped, and those of the second part shaped like an hour-glass, and this visual device is not arbitrary but reflects and answers the movement of the thought and emotion at each point.

Of the more limpid, open-worked poems of the third period, "Poem in October," though written earlier than the others in this group, can stand as an excellent example. The poet, on his thirtieth birthday, is remembering his past and seeing himself in the familiar Welsh landscape as a boy with his mother:

> It was my thirtieth year to heaven
> Woke to my hearing from harbour and neighbour wood
> And the mussel pooled and the heron
> Priested shore
> The morning beckon
> With water praying and call of seagull and rook
> And the knock of sailing boats on the net webbed wall
> Myself to set foot
> That second
> In the still sleeping town and set forth.

Again we have the sacramentalizing of nature ("heron priested shore") and we have also a sense of glory in the natural world which Thomas learned to render more and more effectively as his art matured. Again, one cannot see the quality of the poem from an extract; elegy is combined with remembrance and commemoration, and the emotion rises and falls in a fine movement.

Thomas's radio play, *Under Milk Wood,* was broadcast by the B.B.C. and won instant approval among professional critics and laymen alike. In writing for the radio Thomas naturally avoided any too close packing of the imagery, and chose a style closer to that of "Poem in October" than to that of his earlier poems. In spite of an occasional touch of sentimentality *Under Milk Wood* is a remarkable performance, one of the few examples in our time of spoken poetry[1] which is both good and popular. In estimating the loss to literature caused by Thomas's early death, I should be in-

---

[1] I call the language of *Under Milk Wood* poetry, though it is prose to the *eye.* When I wrote this I had *heard* the play twice but I had not read it, and there is no doubt that to the ear it is poetry. The opposite is true of T. S. Eliot's later plays, where the language is verse to the eye but prose to the ear.

clined to put the cutting short of his career as a poet for the radio as the most serious of all. Thomas was by instinct a popular poet—as he wrote:

> Not for the proud man apart
> From the raging moon I write
> On these spindrift pages
> Nor for the towering dead
> With their nightingales and psalms
> But for the lovers, their arms
> Round the griefs of the ages,
> Who pay no praise or wages
> Nor heed my craft or art.

He had no desire to be difficult or esoteric. He drew on the Bible and on universal folk themes rather than on obscure late classical writers or Jessie Weston's *From Ritual to Romance*. In *Under Milk Wood* he puts into simple yet powerful and cunning words a day in the life of a Welsh village, with each character rendered in terms of some particular human weakness or folly. Unlike Eliot, Thomas accepted man as he was: he had a relish for humanity. By the end of his life he had learned to be both poetically honest and poetically simple—a difficult combination, especially in our time. And in choosing the spoken verse of the radio as a medium he was pointing the way towards a bridging of the appalling gap in our culture between professional critic and ordinary reader.

Was he a great poet? Against him it can be argued that his range was severely limited, that (in his earlier poems) he overdid a handful of images and phrases to the point almost of parodying himself, that many of his poems are clotted with an excess of parallel-seeking metaphors. I doubt if he wrote a dozen really first-rate poems; these would include, among those not hitherto mentioned here, "In the white giant's thigh" and "In country sleep." In his favour it can be claimed that at his best he is magnificent, as well as original in tone and technique, and that he was growing in poetic stature to the last. Perhaps the question is, in the most literal sense, academic. It is enough that he wrote some poems that the world will not willingly let die.

The Welsh Background

by John Ackerman

"One: I am a Welshman; two: I am a drunkard; three: I am a lover of the human race, especially of women." [1] This concise, humorous, and not untruthful account of himself was given by Dylan Thomas to an audience in Rome in 1947. It shows that he was aware of the extent to which his temperament and his imagination were the products of his Welsh environment.

With this remark we may compare two earlier statements made by Thomas: first,

> I hold a beast, an angel, and a madman in me, and my enquiry is as to their working, and my problem is their subjugation and victory, downthrow and upheaval, and my effort is their self-expression; [1]

second,

> Poetry, recording the stripping of the individual darkness, must inevitably cast light upon what has been hidden for too long, and, by so doing, make clean the naked exposure. Freud cast light on a little darkness he had exposed. Benefiting by the sight of the light and the knowledge of the hidden nakedness, poetry must drag further into the clean nakedness of light more even of the hidden causes than Freud could realize. [2]

The tone and substance are apocalyptic, self-conscious and rhetorical, showing the impact of surrealism and Freudian psychology on

[1] Quoted by Geoffrey Moore in "Dylan Thomas," *Kenyon Review*, XVII (Spring 1955), 261.

[2] Dylan Thomas, *New Verse*, No. 11 (October 1934), p. 9. Thomas was then nineteen years old.

a young mind. But they represent attitudes the poet was to outgrow. Dylan Thomas grew "from dragon's tooth to druid in his own land." [3] The movement in his poetry was from a clinical towards a religious purpose.

Writing under the influence of early attitudes, Thomas often dissipated his prodigious energy. His work was too diffuse, and his imagination frequently lacked direction. With an increase in craftsmanship, a growing sense of purpose and dedication as a poet, came a widening, and at the same time a greater control, of theme and form. There is an extension of sympathy and understanding; the use of Christian myth and symbol; the emergence of a poetry of vision. But the potentiality of this development was present in his early work. The achievement represented by *Collected Poems* and *Under Milk Wood* indicates that Thomas, with an increasing sureness of instinct, came to make the best use of his poetic talent.

The progress of a writer depends, however, not only upon his own canalization of his energies, but also upon the prevailing climate of influence and taste. Thomas began publishing in the thirties, but from the beginning he was neither a political nor an intellectual poet. The first impact of *18 Poems* and, two years later, of *Twenty-five Poems,* lay in their originality: they were unlike any other poetry written in English at the time. Certainly there were few affinities with such poets as Auden, Spender, and Empson. His poetry was the product of a strongly individual imagination fostered by ways of thought and feeling Welsh in origin.

The distinctive characteristics of Thomas's work are its lyrical quality, its strict formal control, a romantic conception of the poet's function, and a religious attitude to experience. These are characteristics shared by other Anglo-Welsh writers. They were not qualities particularly current among English writers of the thirties. If we remember the difference between Thomas's use of Christian thought and symbol and T. S. Eliot's we need hardly seek any relationship there. Thomas's ideas derived from a different tradition. "Religion, such as he knew it," writes Karl Shapiro, "was direct and natural; the symbolism of religion, as he uses it, is poetry, direct knowledge. Religion is not to be used: it is simply part of life, part of himself; it is like a tree; take it or leave it, it is there." [4] That is, it was part

---

[3] Gwyn Jones, "Welsh Dylan," *Adelphi*, XXX, No. 2 (February 1954), 115.
[4] Karl Shapiro, "Dylan Thomas," *Poetry*, LXXXVII, No. 2 (November 1955), 105.

of the man; a way of feeling he inherited rather than acquired. The religious element in Thomas's poetry is the key to its correct interpretation. It was the most important result of Welsh influence. "When he said he was a Puritan he was not believed; but it really was true." [5] This fact is central to a full understanding of his work, for Puritanism had long directed Welsh life and thought. Its influence, for better or worse, was inescapable.

II

The Welsh influence was present in three forms. First and foremost, there was the direct and inevitable influence of a particular community with particular traditions. Secondly, there was the influence of other Welshmen writing in English. These Anglo-Welsh writers helped to create a national consciousness, the sense of a life being lived that was peculiar to Wales: with them Thomas discovered a community of ideas and outlook. The third influence present in his environment was the tradition of culture existing in and through the Welsh language. Since he knew no Welsh this influence came through the two channels already mentioned: contact with Welsh-speaking relatives and friends, and through translations of Welsh poetry and prose.

As Geoffrey Moore writes in an article viewing the poet's work against his Welsh environment:

> The national feeling engendered by so many hundreds of years of Welsh speaking survives now without the actual bond of language. The harp of Wales sounds in the ears of Welshmen whether they are archdruids from Bangor or boyos from the back streets of Cardiff. Without being hopelessly mystical about race, one can with some confidence assert that both it and environment have an effect on the nature of a people and the art that springs from them . . . the spirit of place and of country is an inescapable influence. To this degree, and to the degree that Dylan Thomas *opened himself* to the scenes and people and manners of the place in which he was born, it is meaningful to talk about the Welsh quality of his work.[6]

Welsh influence is, inevitably, present in his earliest work, but he was then less aware of it as such. It was when Thomas for the first

---

[5] Vernon Watkins, comment on a review of J. M. Brinnin, *Dylan Thomas in America*, in *Encounter*, VI, No. 6 (June 1956), 78.

[6] Geoffrey Moore, "Dylan Thomas," *Kenyon Review*, XVII (Spring 1955), 264-65.

time moved away from Wales that he began to see its life and traditions in perspective, and realized how they differed from the life
and traditions of England. What was more important, he became
aware of himself as belonging to this native culture, a culture which
was becoming increasingly related to that of England but inescapably of different origin. His parents spoke Welsh, but he himself,
though not Welsh-speaking, knew as much Welsh as do most of the
inhabitants of South Wales. He was familiar with the more common phrases in use and well acquainted with the sound and verbal
music of the Welsh tongue.

In his Note to the *Collected Poems* Thomas wrote:

> I read somewhere of a shepherd who, when asked why he made,
> from within fairy rings, ritual observances to the moon to protect his
> flocks, replied: "I'd be a damn' fool if I didn't!" These poems, with
> all their crudities, doubts, and confusions, are written for the love of
> Man and in praise of God, and I'd be a damn' fool if they weren't.

There is a bardic ring about this statement. Thomas is claiming a
high function for the poet, though as usual there is a "dog among
the fairies" mocking wisdom, which, in the light of such apocalyptic
and romantic claims, is a defensive irony. Frequently in his later
poems he assumes the role of prophet, of a person mediating, in his
art, between man and God. This is so, for example, in "Author's
Prologue" to the *Collected Poems,* "Over Sir John's hill," and
"Poem on his birthday." The poet here is a man endowed with
special wisdom. In his statements about his work Thomas was very
careful to support this myth already created in the poetry. This
high estimation of the poet's place and function derives from
specific traditions of Welsh life and thought. "For in ancient Wales
or Ireland a poet was not merely a professional verse-writer: he was
acknowledged to exercise extraordinary spiritual power." [7] A. G.
Prys-Jones writes:

> These influences had always been in his environment. . . . No one
> who has read his poems or heard him declaim them can fail to recog-
> nize his bardic affinities—or the racial sources of his headlong rhetoric,
> his passionate intensity, his powerful imaginative strength and his
> mystical, religious vision. In one very real sense, he belonged to

[7] Robert Graves, Foreword to Alun Lewis, *Ha! Ha! Among the Trumpets*
(London: George Allen & Unwin, Ltd., 1945), p. 7.

the company of the great pulpit orators of Wales who were often
bards . . .[8]

To this tradition can be attributed, in part, Thomas's confidence
in his romantic and apocalyptic manner. General cultural movements such as surrealism and Freudian theories of art had, at best,
clinical rather than religious or moral pretensions. It was his Welsh
environment which offered a background of thought and culture
fostering belief in the more primitive, mystical, and romantic conception of the poet.

Religion   III

The Welsh eisteddfod, in its present form, was first established in
1789. There was also at that time a renewed interest in the religion
of nature and in the cults of the druids. Iolo Morganwg, who sought
to prove that these traditions had continued unbroken since druidi-
cal times in his native shire of Glamorgan, elaborated a ritual which
purported to belong to the druids. On June 21, 1792, these fabrica-
tions were put into practice when he held the first *gorsedd* or esoteric coterie of bards, and they have been part of the eisteddfod
programme ever since.[9] Therefore from this time in particular, due
to the addition of allegedly primitive rites to the eisteddfod ceremony, certain mystical and recondite powers were attributed to the
bard. Such ideas would obviously please the romantic imagination,
but it must be remembered that the discipline of Welsh bardic
poetry is among the strictest in any known literature. It was written
in elaborate metres, and continues to be to the present day. Herein
lies the paradox of the bardic tradition. The exuberance of the
bardic personality, the liking for ceremony and elaborate ritual, co-
exist with a most craftsmanlike devotion to composition. The picture
of himself that Thomas gave to his public presents an interesting
and not, I think, unrelated parallel. There was on the one hand the
flamboyant, larger-than-life part he played to the world; and on the
other the painstaking pattern and discipline in his verse, which,
during his lifetime, generally passed unnoticed.

---

[8] A. G. Prys-Jones, "Death Shall Have No Dominion," *Dock Leaves* (Dylan
Thomas Memorial Number), V, No. 13 (Spring 1954), 27.
[9] See David Williams, *A History of Modern Wales* (London: John Murray,
Publishers, Ltd., 1950), p. 272.

Another important feature of old Welsh poetry is an awareness of the dual nature of reality, of unity in disunity, of the simultaneity of life and death, of time as an eternal moment rather than as something with a separate past and future. The basis of this is a sense of paradox, or, in slightly different terms, a paradoxical conception of existence. Gwyn Williams, in the Foreword to his collection of early Welsh poetry, writes:

> I have entitled this book *The Burning Tree* to suggest an outstanding mood of the Welsh poet, the awareness at the same time of contrary seasons and passions, a mood in which the poet brings into one phrase the force of love and war, of summer and winter, of holy sacrament and adulterous love.

> Matthew Arnold in his *Study of Celtic Literature* notes a passage from the *Mabinogion* as an instance of what he calls Celtic magic. "And they saw a tall tree by the side of the river, one half of which was in flames from the root to the top, and the other half was green and in full leaf." It was enough for Arnold to recognize this as magic, distinguishing it from the radiant, uncomplicated Greek way of handling nature, without prying into the mechanics of the image. Coleridge might have helped him here, for this Celtic tree is a hitherto unapprehended relation of things, an integration of spring and autumn such as Spenser expressed in a more English way and at greater length in the stanza beginning:

> > There is continuall Spring, and harvest there
> > Continuall, both meeting at one tyme . . .
> > > (*Faerie Queene III.xlii*)

> A similarly startling juxtaposition of the unexpected occurs in Keats's phrase "fairy lands forlorn," which Arnold also quotes and in which he finds the very same note struck. . . . It is the suddenness and success of this linking of the previously held to be incongruous that makes metaphysical poetry and distinguishes Dafydd ap Gwilym from Chaucer, John Donne from Ben Jonson, Dylan Thomas from W. H. Auden.[10]

This introduces an important aspect of Thomas's poetry. A sense of paradox and, derived from this, a liking for the violent yoking of discordant images, a natural tendency to think of things in terms of their opposites, are characteristics of his early work. They direct

[10] Gwyn Williams, *The Burning Tree* (London: Faber and Faber, Ltd., 1956), p. 13.

his method of composition, for it must be remembered that his techniques were the result of a specific attitude to experience. Likewise, the art of composition in Welsh poetry owes much to this apprehension of the duality of existence. The poem itself tends to be a pattern of the experience, but given without a narrative design. Development of "meaning" in the poem is concentric rather than linear. The relationship between the parts is total rather than consecutive, as in Thomas's "Author's Prologue," "Fern Hill," and "Poem in October." It is a whole experience, without actual end or beginning. Since the development of the poem depends to a lesser degree than is usual upon narrative outline or consecutive development of the thought, a greater emphasis is thrown upon formal qualities. The art depends upon a technical rather than intellectual discipline. There is extensive and subtle use of sound and rhythm; repetition of image, rhythm, and phrase; and a frequent use of parallel constructions. Emphasis on formal control often seems a substitute for intellectual application. Thomas, similarly, builds up his poems from an elaborate sound-structure, the basis of which is the stanza form. Such elaborate use of the stanza as he makes in "Poem in October" and "Fern Hill" is an example of his technical innovation as a poet. He was always as meticulously attentive to the sound of the words as to their meaning. There is evidence of this in his reviews of other poets.

I have stressed the importance of sound in Welsh poetry, and the consequent use of an elaborate prosody, but it must be remembered that this high estimation of the music of the verse does not preclude profundity or significance of content. It has few affinities with Swinburnian rhetoric. Thomas Parry in his *History of Welsh Literature* observed:

> It is important here to recall the critical standpoint which determined Welsh poetry down to the end of the eighteenth century . . . *That standpoint is that sound is as important as sense; that metre and* cynghanedd, *the whole framework of verse, are as much a part of the aesthetic effect as what is said.** . . . The tendency of modern criticism has been to consider primarily the thought expressed in a poem; as for the rhythm, the rhymes, the alliteration, they are desirable no doubt but are regarded as an adornment of the verse. . . .[11]

[11] Thomas Parry, *A History of Welsh Literature,* trans. by H. Idris Bell (London: Oxford University Press, 1955), p. 48.

Parry adds in a footnote:

> This paragraph is so vital to a proper appreciation, and even to any
> real understanding, of Welsh bardic poetry that I have ventured to
> italicize the above sentence.* It is worth mentioning that Welsh
> criticism distinguishes *cerdd dafod* ("tongue song," i.e. poetry) and
> *cerdd dant* ("string song," i.e. music). Both are *cerdd*, song.

The word *cynghanedd* means harmony, and in poetry is a means of
giving pattern to a line by the echoing of sounds, consonantal and
vowel. There are three main divisions of *cynghanedd: cynghanedd
gytsain* consists of multiple alliteration; *cynghanedd sain* has alliteration and rhyme within the line; and *cynghanedd lusg* has in-
ternal rhyme only. An instance of *cynghanedd sain* in English would
be: "The road with its load of lads," where "road" rhymes with
"load," and the "l" of "load" is repeated in "lads." [12]
The critic, when documenting the metrical patterns in Welsh
poetry, approaches them from the outside. It would be misleading
to think of the poet as working in a like manner. The bards were
trained over a long period to use complex verbal patterns of sound
and meaning. Hence it probably became an instinctive way of shaping their thought and feeling. It would be wrong to think of them
labouring consciously for every alliteration, every thread in the
pattern. Obviously the words, with their appropriate metrical relationships, often came unconsciously to the poet. Then he finished
the pattern and coordinated the metrics of the stanza. Sound and
image begin as an instinctive, natural impulse and it is only in the
final organization of the parts that rational control enters. The
poet's knowledge of the patterns of composition would, to some extent, subconsciously direct his writing. It is necessary to appreciate
this fact in order to see Thomas's relationship to the Welsh metrical
tradition in its right perspective. Obviously a rhythm, a sequence
of sounds—such as "young and easy," "Adam and maiden," "green
and golden" from "Fern Hill"—came to him separately, as a number of images might come. These Thomas builds into a longer sequence of verbal patterns (a whole poem) by conscious craftsmanship. Having begun with one rhythm he modifies it, starts another,
goes back to the first, forming them into a pattern of sounds. I
think it probable that in consciously organizing this structure of

[12] See Gwyn Williams, *An Introduction to Welsh Poetry* (London, Faber and
Faber, Ltd., 1953), pp. 243-45.

sound, he was aware of precedent for his patterns in Welsh poetry. An analysis of the sound-structure of "Fern Hill" shows how Thomas employs some of the techniques peculiar to Welsh prosody. In the latter there is a more elaborate and organic sound-structure than is usual in English poetry. Gwyn Jones considers Thomas to be "Welsh in the cunning complexity of his metres, not only in the loose *cynghanedd,* the chime of consonants and pealing vowels, but in the relentless discipline of his verse." [13]

In his essay on Welsh literature Matthew Arnold notes the emphasis on technique in Welsh verse:

> the true art, the *architectonicé* which shapes great works, such as the *Agamemnon* or the *Divine Comedy,* comes only after a steady, deep-searching survey, a firm conception of the facts of human life, which the Celt has not patience for. So he runs off into technic, where he employs the utmost elaboration, and attains astonishing skill; but in the contents of his poetry you have only so much interpretation of the world as the first dash of a quick, strong perception, and then sentiment, infinite sentiment, can bring you.[14]

This is a censure which could be applied equally to twentieth century Anglo-Welsh poetry and prose, with the possible exception of Thomas's own, where mastery of technique became increasingly allied to imaginative vision.

As a consequence of this technical dexterity, linked to a quick and strong perception, the distinctive quality of Welsh poetry is style. This aspect of Welsh literature Matthew Arnold also commented upon:

> This something is *style,* and the Celts certainly have it in a wonderful measure. Style is the most striking quality of their poetry . . . by throwing all its force into style, by bending language at any rate to its will, and expressing the ideas it has with unsurpassable intensity, elevation, and effect.[15]

The success of Thomas's work is also primarily one of style: his language is vigorous and exciting; his ideas impress because of the intensity and elevation with which they are expressed. From the beginning his genius lay more in stylistic than intellectual original-

[13] Gwyn Jones, "Welsh Dylan," *Adelphi,* XXX, No. 2 (Spring 1954), 115.
[14] Matthew Arnold, *On the Study of Celtic Literature* (London: J. M. Dent and Sons, 1919), p. 83.
[15] *Ibid.,* p. 110.

ity. The ideas informing his work are sometimes few and repetitive, but it is the force and subtlety with which they are expressed that is remarkable. Likewise, since one of the distinctive qualities of Thomas's poetry is its emphasis on technique, his development as a poet is characterized, in particular, by an increasing technical craftsmanship. The consummate artistry of the later poems is in the tradition, whether by accident or design, of Welsh verse.

IV

Welsh Nonconformity, since it stressed the importance of "personal salvation" and was concerned with the personal relationship between man, as an individual, and God, created a climate of intense and introspective religious fervour. It also encouraged the reading of the Bible. Two important characteristics of Welsh life at the beginning of the twentieth century were therefore determined: the presence of an articulate, religious people; and in them the existence of an introspective, Puritan and, at its most fertile, divided conscience. The Bible is a most important influence in Anglo-Welsh writing, and is the source of a great part of Thomas's imagery. Likewise the Nonconformist ethic, in its concern with the individual conscience, sin, and salvation, provides the moral tension that characterizes his work.

The popularity of the new religious movement was also due, undoubtedly, to its emotional appeal. The preaching festivals, the frequent impassioned revivals, and the great feasts of hymn-singing provided an emotional and passionate people with the excitement and inspiration that their hard lives otherwise denied them. Welsh hymn singing possessed the *hiraeth,* the other-worldly aspiration of an ancient race. Geraint Goodwin, in his novel, *The Heyday in the Blood,* has evoked the strange, yearning, overpowering emotion at the heart of Welsh hymn-singing:

> And then, like the wind gathering in a howl, came the slow, unearthly cadences of a hymn; it began, slow, inevitable, gathering strength just as the wind; as wild and pitiless as the wind. It had no place, like the wind. It began and it ended, but it gave nothing. It went in a whine, in fury, overhead, to the unreachable places. The human voice that had gone into it had become lost; the hymn had absorbed it, had taken it as the earth takes in its own growth. The

hymn was beyond the choir, . . . beyond them all. It was like some
dark, clouded flame, leaping up in its sombre beauty, remote and
pure.[16]

The solitariness and the passion of Welsh hymnology are born of,
and answer, a profound need in the Welsh character. One is reminded of Caitlin Thomas's comment on a service held after her
husband's death:

> I shall never forget, after that futile church service: a mealy-mouthed
> compromise between literary preciosity and the overriding fear of
> making fools of themselves by too much musical pomp and ritual:
> when Dylan would have obviously preferred the typical blood and
> thunder Welsh hymns passionately shouted over him.[17]

From the Nonconformist movement came "the great preachers
of Wales, the seasonal preaching congresses reminiscent of bardic
meetings, and that singing or chanting eloquence known as *hwyl*." [18]
This is a manner of speech much used by Welsh preachers, both in
Welsh and English, and much loved by their congregations. T. Rowland Hughes, the Welsh novelist, has thus defined it:

> In preaching, or extempore prayer, sometimes even in descriptive
> speech, the speaker, under stress of emotion or deep conviction, in-
> stinctively and unconsciously lapses into this form of fervent declara-
> tion, which makes an instant appeal to the hearts of Welshmen.[19]

The chapel, while it maintained its control of Wales, shaped the
Welsh temperament to a greater extent than the school; and it is
not surprising that Anglo-Welsh writers should have found the influence of the pulpit an immediate one. Made sensitive, under its
ever-present influence, to the sound of words, such a writer as
Thomas found rhythm, incantation, the music of the line (whether
in prose or verse) basic aids to expression.

An interesting example of the way in which Nonconformist,
radical, and popular sympathies in Welsh life tend to unite is found

---

[16] Geraint Goodwin, *The Heyday in the Blood* (London: Penguin Books, 1954),
p. 124.
[17] Caitlin Thomas, *Leftover Life to Kill* (London: Putnam and Co., Ltd., 1957),
pp. 73-74.
[18] Rhys Davies, *The Story of Wales* (London: William Collins Sons and Co.,
Ltd., 1943), p. 24.
[19] T. Rowland Hughes, *From Hand to Hand*, trans. from the Welsh by R. C.
Ruck (London: Methuen and Co., Ltd. 1950), p. 27.

in the career of William Thomas, 1834-79. William Thomas was the brother of Dylan's paternal grandfather. He would seem to be celebrated in Dylan's middle name, Marlais, for he wrote under the name of Gwilym Marles, this being probably an older form of Marlais. Gwilym Marles came from north Carmarthen, as do both sides of Thomas's family, and Marlais is the name of a small river in Carmarthenshire. Gwilym Marles became a Unitarian minister in Cardiganshire, writing both poetry and prose in Welsh. He was especially famous for his radical writings, being a liberal in theology and a radical in politics, and was expelled from his living on account of his radical teaching.

I have outlined some of the traditions of the environment in which Thomas and his contemporaries grew up, and about which they were later to write. Of these eloquent and silver-tongued intruders into English literature, Gwyn Jones has written that "this was the last generation that paid for emergence with its fathers' sweat and bruises; bible-blest and chapel-haunted, wrestle hard as we can, we stand confessed the last, lost nonconformists of an Age." [20] The picture of Thomas as a lost Nonconformist, "bible-blest and chapel-haunted," wrestling with an inherited religion, is certainly closer to the truth than many others that have been offered of him.

V

The twentieth century has seen the decline of Welsh as the first language of Wales, and increasing numbers of Welshmen today speak only English. The period following the 1914-18 War saw the emergence of Welshmen writing in English, among them Dylan Thomas, who had little in common with English literary movements in the inter-war years. They were a different people, conscious of a different tradition. In his editorial to the first number of the *Welsh Review*, February 1939, Gwyn Jones writes:

It is perhaps the most spectacular manifestation of the mental activity of the district [South Wales] that the last few years have seen the emergence of a group of young writers (young in age or work) who for the first time are interpreting Wales to the outside world.

[20] Gwyn Jones, Introduction to *Welsh Short Stories* (London: Oxford University Press, 1956), p. xiii.

They can be called a school only in the sense that Welsh blood, sometimes thickened to a mongrel brew, flows in their veins. They are as diverse as the land that gave them their rich if ragged heritage, but I believe firmly that they will soon be recognized as the most valuable leaven in English literature since the Irishmen opened insular eyes at the beginning of the century.

These notable intruders include Caradoc Evans, Dylan Thomas, Gwyn Jones, Vernon Watkins, Alun Lewis, R. S. Thomas, Gwyn Thomas, and Glyn Jones. They produce their best work when writing about Wales and the life they have known there. But it is a quality of style—fierce enthusiasm, energy and flexibility—that links and most distinguishes them. Other characteristics are a richness of metaphor, often not as precise or consistent as it might be; a dominantly sensuous, often sensual imagination; a delight in fantasy and the irrational; and a deep, pervading pathos. They begin with the word or phrase rather than the idea: their approach, even in prose, is that of the poet, and they tend to convey their meaning through the medium of the senses. This aptitude for sensory communication, combined with a Welsh inclination to eloquence and a natural tendency to speak in metaphor, can all too easily result in loose and high-flown rhetoric. However, a robust sense of humour and a liking for strict formal control guard against this disposition.

Another feature of Anglo-Welsh writing is that it tends to be subjective, and consequently introspective. It is characterized by permanent romantic attitudes: a posited belief in intuition, in the vitality of strong and passionate emotions, and in the influence of external nature. Its favourite themes are the exploration of childhood, death, and the sexual nature of man. We find also a conscious cultivation of the primitive, and a strong vein of comedy, based on observation of the more humorous aspects of Welsh life. The Anglo-Welsh writer, both in poetry and prose, moved away from interest in the sophisticated and intellectual. Thomas was aware of this tendency among his contemporaries. Stephen Spender, in his review of Thomas's *Collected Poems,* said:

> Dylan Thomas represents a romantic revolt against this classicist tendency which has crystallized around the theological views of Eliot and Auden. It is a revolt against more than this, against the Oxford, Cambridge and Harvard intellectualism of much modern poetry in the English language; against the King's English of London and the South,

which has become a correct idiom capable of refinements of beauty, but incapable of harsh effects, coarse texture and violent colours.[21]

Thomas wrote: ". . . this is now the clearest, most considered and sympathetic, and, in my opinion, truest review that I have ever seen of my writing. I mean, that your statement and understanding of my aim and method seems to me altogether true." [22]

In this outline of Welsh influences and relationships in Thomas's work, it is also important to consider certain theological concepts which inform much Anglo-Welsh poetry. These ideas have shaped the religious attitude to experience. In particular, the celebration by the poet of all natural life, animal and vegetal, a celebration expressed usually in sensuous terms, is derived from specific theological concepts. The basis of this attitude is a sense of the unity of all creation, and this identity of all created forms is religious in character. The poet is aware of a sacramental universe in which the common things of life serve to illustrate profound mysteries. Hence all created things, whether blades of grass or sea-waves breaking on to the shore or "the fishing holy stalking heron," are of themselves holy and are a witness to the Creator.

There is a Hebraic element in the Welsh character—probably the result of much Bible reading—from which stems the belief that everything in the world is, for its own sake, holy. "They [the Welsh] did not like it when I told them the Welsh would make Hebrews of themselves very soon, if they didn't take to some other book than the Bible," observed Edward Thomas in a letter written from Ammanford, Carmarthen. Platonic notions of the Idea behind external objects have, it might be claimed, hindered English poetry and English Christianity far too much. In the Hebraic conception of life each object is in itself holy. Each is part of a sacramental whole, not an imitation of some idea. Thus we have the peculiar "inscape" and "instress" of Hopkins, who sought the reality of each external object; for things exist and are important as they are, not as images of an ideal form. Hopkins's "reality" was expressed in sensuous language that attempted to define the physical actuality of the thing. A concept of reality where every natural object contains the divine is obviously congenial to poetic creation. The Welsh character possesses a feeling of awe, a sense of the wonder of creation, to which is

[21] Stephen Spender, *Spectator* (December 5, 1952), pp. 780-81.
[22] Letter to Stephen Spender (December 9, 1952), quoted in Derek Stanford, *Dylan Thomas* (London: Neville Spearman, Ltd., 1954), p. 25.

allied a sensitivity towards external nature and a sense of pristine innocence. In the formulation of this attitude to reality, contemporary Anglo-Welsh writers, including Dylan Thomas, have been influenced also by the work of Blake. When reading Thomas's poetry one is reminded constantly of Blake's "For everything that lives is holy, life delights in life."

The years 1900-36 brought South Wales into the main stream of world protest against poverty, inequality, and industrial materialism. The region produced one of the most intense expressions of revolt against the existing social order. The enthusiasm which had been aroused a few years earlier by the frequent religious revivals (*diwygiad*) was now turned to politics and literature. Gwyn Thomas has eloquently recalled the environment that fostered the South Wales writer in the twenties and thirties:

> Those Rhondda days are, for me, for ever bathed in a brilliant light; the tumult of political enthusiasms, the white-hot oratory of the people's paladins, the festivals of folk singing and hymn singing in the vast chapels, moving groups on the hillsides at night . . . their echoes can still fill my mind with an intense creative excitement. Then the hill-walks across to Llanwonno, or over to the Dimbath, the Beacons to the north, pulling us towards an even wilder solitude than we had ever known; and the Vale of Glamorgan to the South, tempting us to an ordered placidity which it would benefit our souls to cultivate. And between these two poles of attraction, the fermenting disquiet of the Valley streets, ringing with every note of pain and laughter contrived since man's beginning. In that small territory of land and feeling lay the whole world's experience. The years of study and experiment have driven convenient lines of communication through it; they have not enlarged its frontiers nor enriched the texture of its earth.[23]

Dylan Thomas remarked that

> out of the mining valleys of South Wales, there were poets who were beginning to write in a spirit of passionate anger against the inequality of social conditions. They wrote, not of the truths and beauties of the natural world, but of the lies and ugliness of the unnatural system of society under which they worked—or, more often during the nineteen-twenties and thirties, under which they were not allowed to work.[24]

---

[23] Gwyn Thomas, quoted in Gwyn Jones, "Language, Style, and the Anglo-Welsh," *Essays and Studies* (London: John Murray, Publishers, Ltd., 1953), p. 107.
[24] Dylan Thomas, *Quite Early One Morning* (London: J. M. Dent and Sons, 1954), pp. 147-48.

Poets spoke, Thomas continues,

> in ragged angry rhythms, of the Wales *they* knew: the coal-tips, the
> dole-queues, the stubborn bankrupt villages, the children, scrutting for
> coal on the slag-heaps, the colliers' shabby allotments, the cheap-jack
> cinema, the whippet races, the disused quarries, the still pit-wheels
> . . . silicosis, little Moscow up beyond the hills.[25]

He probably had in mind Alun Lewis's poem "The Mountain Over
Aberdare" when he wrote this passage.[26]

The Anglo-Welsh writer found in South Wales at this time a
background of creative vitality and social ferment. In his own work,
however, Thomas was primarily concerned not with political, but
with emotional, religious, and sexual man.

VI

To its first readers, Thomas's poetry seemed strange and difficult
because they came to it with tastes developed by contemporary literature, and a knowledge of twentieth century literature offered little aid to its understanding. The language and ideas to be found in
Thomas's work had little in common with the imagery and ideas in

[25] *Ibid.*, p. 148.
[26] Alun Lewis, "The Mountain Over Aberdare," from *Raiders' Dawn* (London:
George Allen & Unwin, Ltd., 1942), p. 87:

> From this high quarried ledge I see
> The place for which the Quakers once
> Collected clothes, my fathers' home,
> Our stubborn bankrupt village sprawled
> In jaded dust beneath its nameless hills;
> The drab streets strung across the cwm,
> Derelict workings, tips of slag
> The gospellers and gamblers use
> And children scrutting for the coal
> That winter dole cannot purvey;
> Allotments where the collier digs
> While engines hack the coal within his brain;
> Grey Hebron in a rigid cramp,
> White cheap-jack cinema, the church
> Stretched like a sow beside the stream;
> And mourners in their Sunday best
> Holding a tiny funeral, singing hymns
> That drift insidious as the rain. . . .
>
> And in a curtained parlour women hug
> Huge grief, and anger against God. . . .

the work of, say, W. H. Auden, T. S. Eliot or W. B. Yeats. Neither did it derive, to any great extent, from the nineteenth century romantic poets. "No poet of the English language had so hoodwinked and confuted his critics. None has ever worn more brilliantly the mask of anarchy to conceal the true face of tradition. . . . The most mistaken of his admirers were those who loved it [the poetry] for its novelty." [27] The Anglo-Welsh writer A. G. Prys-Jones has suggested where this tradition lies: "He was far more at home, I think, with Vaughan and Traherne, Blake . . . than with Freud and Marx, Kafka, Joyce and Proust." [28] Indeed, contemporary Anglo-Welsh writing generally has been influenced by the religious poets of the seventeenth century. Thomas in particular has several important features in common with them: an interest in childhood as a state of innocence and grace; a deep sense of guilt and of separation from God, alternating with moments of vision; a liking for wit and paradox; and the use of Christian imagery and symbolism.

Dylan Thomas, like Donne, speaks with directness and passion on the theme of sex. His work shows the same mingling of sexual and religious themes, which results in a mingling of sexual and religious imagery. In both poets there is an intense consciousness of death. Donne preached a sermon, *Deaths Duell*, in his grave-clothes, and Thomas's poems show a similar obsession with the physical fact of death:

> I sit and watch the worm beneath my nail
> Wearing the quick away.[29]

In the analysis of Thomas's poems we shall find specific sources of theme and image in the work of Donne, and Thomas also is preoccupied with the relationship of divine and sexual love.

An important area of sensibility shared by the Anglo-Welsh poets of the twentieth century and the metaphysical poets of the seventeenth, one alien to the Romantic period, is the religious attitude to experience. This produced a poetry characterized by religious conflict and, on the positive side, religious vision. The religious mysticism in the work of Vaughan, Traherne, or Thomas is very differ-

[27] Vernon Watkins, "Innovation and Tradition," unsigned Obituary Notice, *The Times* (November 10, 1953).
[28] A. G. Prys-Jones, "Death Shall Have No Dominion," *Dock Leaves*, V, No. 13 (Spring 1954), 26.
[29] *Collected Poems*, p. 13.

ent from the mystical aspiration in the poetry of Wordsworth or
Shelley. The keen introspective analysis and extreme subjectivity
which the seventeenth century poets brought into literature is often
revealed most satisfyingly in the poetry of religious vision.

The main characteristic of the introspective consciousness, then
as today, is a profound sense of division, which reveals itself in various forms. Renan attributed to the Celt a defiance of all that comes
from without; an unwillingness to acknowledge the reality of the objective universe. This is apt to express itself in literature by escape
from reality into mysticism, longing, or romance. In Donne, Herbert, Traherne, Vaughan, and Thomas the introspective consciousness is characterized by a deep sense of sin and of separation from
God. Donne's Holy Sonnets, Herbert's *The Temple,* Thomas's "Altarwise by owl-light," "There was a Saviour," and "Vision and
Prayer," all record the attempt to heal this separation.

Expression of the sense of separation, however, sometimes takes a
different form, one that is less directly religious. It is a feeling of
distance from the original innocence of childhood, and a desire to
recapture the lost visionary moments of that time of grace.

> Happy those early dayes! when I
> Shin'd in my Angell-infancy.
> Before I understood this place
> Appointed for my second race . . .
>
> But (ah!) my soul with too much stay
> Is drunk, and staggers in the way.
> Some men a forward motion love,
> But I by backward steps would move,
> And when this dust falls to the urn
> In that state I came return.[30]

Traherne, in his *Centuries of Meditations,* writes of childhood:

All appeared new, and strange at first, inexpressibly rare and de-
lightful and beautiful. I was a little stranger, which at my entrance
into the world was saluted and surrounded with innumerable joys.
My knowledge was divine. I knew by intuition those things which
since my Apostasy, I collected again by the highest reason. My very
ignorance was advantageous. I seemed as one brought into the Estate

[30] L. C. Martin, ed., *The Works of Henry Vaughan,* I (London: Oxford University Press, 1957), 419-20.

of Innocence. All things were spotless and pure and glorious: yea, and infinitely mine, and joyful and precious. I knew not that there were any sins, or complaints or laws. . . . I saw all in the peace of Eden; Heaven and Earth did sing my Creator's praises, and could not make more melody to Adam, than to me. All Time was Eternity, and a perpetual Sabbath. . . .[31]

In this passage, the sentence "and Earth did sing my Creator's praises, and could not make more melody to Adam," suggests that the author has the perception and privilege of the original Adam. Thomas often similarly assumes the identity of Adam or Christ in his poetry and prose. Extreme dependence on the experience of childhood, and the desire to recreate it is a major characteristic of both Anglo-Welsh poetry and prose. In such poems as "Fern Hill" and "Poem in October," this theme finds perhaps, in our own day, its most intense and beautiful expression.

VII

The Anglo-Welsh poet whose work bears the closest relationship to that of Dylan Thomas is Vernon Watkins. Both have certain bardic qualities: they assume a prophetic role, an intuitive knowledge of existence. The eloquent language, religious (but not exclusively Christian) imagery, and rhetorical sweep of the verse, add to this impression of the bardic poet. Vernon Watkins, like W. B. Yeats and Dylan Thomas, reads his poetry aloud in a forceful, chanting manner. The music of the verse is given full value, unlike the fashionable kind of reading satirized by Thomas: "There is the other reader, of course, who manages, by studious flatness, semi-detachment, and an almost condescending undersaying of his poems, to give the impression that what he really means is: Great things, but my own." [32]

Linked with this bardic quality there is, in both poets, a fundamentally religious conception of existence. "In our approach to poetry," writes Vernon Watkins, "and in our method of composition we were unlike, but in our belief and findings there was a great af-

---

[31] Thomas Traherne, *Centuries of Meditations* (London: Bertram Dobell, 1908), pp. 156-57.

[32] Dylan Thomas, "On Reading One's Own Poems," in *Quite Early One Morning,* p. 131.

finity, and we became close friends." [33] Where poetic technique is concerned there are, as Watkins claims, important points of difference—though there are, too, some interesting similarities—but undoubtedly Watkins's work had a most important influence on Thomas's development. They first met after the publication of *18 Poems.* From this time each regularly discussed his work with the other, and their close friendship lasted until Thomas's death.

I have said that Thomas came increasingly to think of himself as a religious poet. It is interesting to find Watkins remarking that

> a comparison between this early version [of the poem "Unluckily for a Death"] which appeared, with two adjectival changes, in *Life and Letters Today* (October 1939) and the poem printed in *Deaths and Entrances* and finally in *Collected Poems* shows that all the changes made in its rewriting were movements away from ironical, and towards religious, statement.[34]

This movement characterizes the development of Thomas's poetry as a whole. Watkins has claimed that both he and Thomas sought a metaphysical truth in their work: for both poets natural observation was significant only in so far as it supported some deeper truth. In the Introduction to his edition of the letters he received from Thomas, Watkins states that his own themes were close to Thomas's, that they

> were both religious poets . . . He [Thomas] understood, too, why I could never write a poem dominated by time, as Hardy could. This, in fact, was also true of Dylan, though some critics have mistakenly thought to find such poems in his work. It illustrates our affinity on a deeper level: his poems spoke to me with the voice of metaphysical truth; if we disagreed it was on a metaphysical issue, for natural observation in poetry meant nothing to us without the support of metaphysical truth.[35]

It was Watkins's personality and work which aided Thomas in his search for an expression of faith which escaped the domination of time.

[33] Vernon Watkins, a short autobiographical note in Stanley J. Kunitz, ed., *Twentieth Century Authors,* First Supplement (New York: H. W. Wilson Co., 1955), p. 1,052.
[34] Dylan Thomas, *Letters to Vernon Watkins* (London: J. M. Dent and Sons and Faber and Faber, 1957), p. 64.
[35] *Ibid.,* pp. 17-18.

The Universe of the Early Poems

by Elder Olson

Dylan Thomas's first book, *18 Poems,* appeared in 1934 and was followed two years later by *Twenty-five Poems.* The contents and the techniques of the two volumes were similar in many respects; the critical reactions to these volumes, with a few exceptions, were similar also. Critics, favorable or unfavorable, found the poetry difficult, irrational, and undisciplined, but also thought it sufficiently important to demand emphatic comment. H. G. Porteus called the poetry "an unconducted tour of bedlam." Louis MacNeice decided that it was wild but rhythmical drunken speech. Stephen Spender made the categorical pronouncement that it was "just poetic stuff with no beginning or end, or intelligent and intelligible control."

Yet, had the poetry of Thomas been such, indeed had it been such and nothing more, one may doubt whether it would have been singled out for special notice. By 1934 there could scarcely have been anything remarkable about a writer whose works were irrational and undisciplined. Movements such as dadaism and surrealism had notoriously forsworn reason and discipline as vices, and the spate of works produced by dadaists and surrealists was quite sufficient to drown eighteen poems by a relatively unknown artist. What was remarkable about the poetry of Thomas was that it had its effect even before it was understood, and sometimes even when it was misunderstood. The very minimum of the effect, moreover, left the reader with the impression that a poet with a remarkable sense of language and rhythm was saying something important about subjects of importance; at the very worst, he had somehow botched his statement by his violence and obscurity.

There was a further characteristic which distinguished Thomas's work from that of other poets. It was unclassifiable. Its "themes," in so far as they could be grasped at all, were the age-old ones of birth, sex, and death, but they were conceived and treated in a way that was anything but familiar. In an age which was beginning to discuss myth and symbol as universalizing all human experience, this poetry used myth so private and symbol so special that it had the effect of recording unique experiences. The age was beginning to demand that poetry have social reference; the poetry of Thomas, quite obviously, had no social reference. The age was acquiring the habit of considering and judging poetry in terms of the tradition that had given rise to it; the poetry of Thomas was apparently unrelated to any tradition. The age was fond of explicating obscure poetry; the poetry of Thomas was so obscure that no one could explicate it.

For what was to be done about a poet who wrote lines like these?

> Altarwise by owl-light in the half-way house
> The gentleman lay graveward with his furies;
> Abaddon in the hangnail cracked from Adam,
> And, from his fork, a dog among the fairies,
> The atlas-eater with a jaw for news,
> Bit out the mandrake with to-morrow's scream. . . .[1]

Edith Sitwell, in a highly appreciative review,[2] sought to interpret these lines and thereby not merely engaged herself in some controversy but provoked the following reproof from the poet himself:

Miss Edith Sitwell's analysis . . . of the lines "The atlas-eater with a jaw for news / Bit out the mandrake with to-morrow's scream" seems to me a bit vague. She says the lines refer to "the violent speed and the sensation-loving, horror-loving craze of modern life." She doesn't take the literal meaning: that a world-devouring ghost-creature bit out the horror of to-morrow from a gentleman's loins. A "jaw for news" is an obvious variation of a "nose for news," and means that the mouth of the creature can taste already the horror that has not yet come, or can sense its coming, can thrust its tongue into news that has not yet been made, can savour the enormity of the progeny before the seed stirs, can realize the crumbling of dead flesh before the opening of the womb that delivers that flesh to to-morrow. What is this creature? It's the dog among the fairies, the rip and cur among the myths, the snapper at demons, the scarer of ghosts, the wizard's heel-chaser. This

[1] *The Collected Poems of Dylan Thomas* (Norfolk, Conn.: New Directions, 1953), p. 80.
[2] *Sunday Times* (London), 1936, cited in Henry Treece, *Dylan Thomas* (London: Lindsay Drummond, 1949), p. 145.

poem is a particular incident in a particular adventure, not a general, elliptical deprecation of this "horrible, crazy, speed-life." [3]

How seriously, one may well ask, are we to take the poet's insistence—an oft-repeated one—that his poetry be read literally? If his interpretation of these lines is a literal one, as it presumably is, how literal is it; and how shall we interpret his interpretation? If it is not literal in the strict sense of the term, in what sense is it so?

If we begin by considering the relation of Thomas's paraphrase to the lines in question, certain things are evident at once. "World-devouring" paraphrases "atlas-eater"; but an atlas is not literally the world. If we are to understand "atlas" as standing for "world," we can do so only by first understanding a geographic atlas as representing the world. Similarly with the adaptation of "a nose for news" into "a jaw for news"; such a jaw becomes a possibility only if we equate "news" with the latest events or happenings, as in fact we do in the conventions of ordinary conversation. So, too, with "mandrake" for "horror"; the mandrake is a horror only in the conventions of witchcraft. In short, the relation of the paraphrase to the verses can be seen only if we observe that Thomas is describing things by reference to other things which, in one convention or another, are their representatives or surrogates.

This is scarcely literal language in the ordinary sense, as the reader can easily assure himself by attempting to determine, after Thomas's "literal" exposition, precisely what the "dog among the fairies" is. Is the diction, then, metaphorical? If we take metaphor as the substitution of names made warrantable by a resemblance between the things signified by the names—that is, as the putting of the name of *A* for that of *B*, on the ground that *A* resembles *B*, or seems to—we can scarcely suppose that Thomas's lines are metaphorical. An atlas of maps does not much *resemble* the world. A person unacquainted with maps would be quite baffled by one, I think, until he had some instruction in the conventions of cartography.

There is this besides: that in understanding metaphor we perceive the substitution of names by keeping the things themselves, or the ideas of them, entirely distinct. If I speak of a man as "a lion in battle," I do not suppose that a lion is a man or that the idea of a lion is the same as the idea of a man. I simply substitute words, on the ground that the man resembles a lion in certain ways. I keep the

[3] Treece, *op. cit.*, p. 149.

idea of man constant, and merely augment certain human attributes to the degree in which a lion is supposed to possess them.

A metaphor, then, involves verbal substitution merely, whereas in these lines of Thomas's we have the *idea* of atlas substituted for the *idea* of world because an atlas is a cartographic representation of the world; the use of the word is merely a consequence of a conceptual substitution which has already occurred. In short, we have here, not metaphor, but symbolism.

We must beware at this point. First of all, there is a general tendency in contemporary discussion of art to assume that all art is symbolic. If the point of this is that a few strokes of the painter's brush are not really a cat, but still represent a cat; that a block of granite, chiseled a bit, is not really Venus, but represents Venus; that the tones of Chopin's "B Flat Minor Sonata," as it first bursts upon us, are not themselves agitated, but somehow represent agitation; if this is what is meant, we shall all agree at once—but reserve the right to think the observation a somewhat obvious one. If the point is that art must be symbolic simply because it *must* be symbolic, we may well ask: how do you know until you have looked? Suppose we grant that all art is symbolic; what is the difference between poetry which really *can* be read literally and the poetry of Dylan Thomas? What is the difference between "Tintern Abbey" or the "Ode to a Nightingale" and the portion of Thomas's "Altarwise by owl-light" sonnet just quoted?

One generally finds, moreover, that those who assume that all art is symbolic will assume, as having absolute force, some universal symbolic system, such as that afforded by the Freudian or Jungian psychology. The consequence of such an assumption is that the value or meaning of the symbol is known before the symbol is inspected in its context. There is some warrant for this position, I suppose, in that any attempt to set forth a symbolic system must perforce assign certain values to the symbols under certain conditions; but the view that symbols have a fixed and unconditional value, or even function in all cases as symbols, is expressly disavowed by both Freud and Jung. What is more important, it is contrary to fact.

That it is contrary to fact in the present instance can be seen at once. Thomas "admitted to the influence" of Freud;[4] but the reader

---

[4] This admission has been widely reported—it appears even on the dust jacket of the *Collected Poems;* but I have been unable to locate it. Perhaps it was made orally; if the remarks made in answer to an inquiry by Geoffrey Grigson (*New Verse,* No. 11, October, 1934, pp. 8-9) are intended, they are very far from

who seeks to interpret the symbols of Thomas in terms of Freud is
not likely to find the poetry very clear. Such a reader will be grati-
fied, no doubt, to observe that Thomas speaks of "the forest of the
loin," [5] that he frequently connects birth with an emergence from
water,[6] and in a few other matters appears to conform to the Freudian symbolic. But the negative instances will quickly diminish that
gratification. Whereas, for Freud, fruit symbolizes the female breast
and definitely does not symbolize offspring, it is generally a child-
symbol for Thomas (as indeed it is in common discourse). Whereas,
for Freud, caves, churches, and chapels refer to the female genitalia,
Thomas uses caves to signify the innermost recesses of the self, and
churches and chapels—particularly sunken ones—to signify lost pristine faiths. Thomas associates ladders and climbing, not with sexual
intercourse, but with man's spiritual ascent. The reader who has the
Jungian archetypes in mind is likely to fare no better, although the
experiences with which Thomas deals are archetypal enough; and,
much as Thomas is concerned with the experience of birth, the
reader who proceeds in terms of the Rankian theory of the birth-
trauma is in an excellent way to miss the whole tendency of the poems; indeed, even to miss Thomas's declared purpose in his art.

It is folly to pretend to interpret what anyone says before you
have listened to what he has to say; it is worse folly to declare what
a work of art must be before you have observed what it is. If universal symbolic systems had unconditional validity, there would be no
problem of interpreting Thomas, or any poet. In Thomas's case his
symbols, far from yielding to the easy key of a ready-made symbology, demand close inspection, and ultimately yield their meaning
only when the reader, by an act of intuition, recognizes the particular derivation of the symbol.

What, for instance, is the meaning of

> The twelve triangles of the cherub wind? [7]

The reader who approaches this with symbolic presupposition is
likely to remain baffled; I will spare you the psychological wildernesses into which he would be led. If, on the other hand, he simply
thinks about winds a bit, he is likely to remember the tradition of

---

any such admission. Thomas's words are: "It [poetry] must drag further into the
clean nakedness of light more even of the hidden causes than Freud could realize."
    [5] *Collected Poems,* p. 6.
    [6] E.g., *ibid.,* pp. 35, 41-44, 49-50, 54-55, 63, 65, 78-79.
    [7] *Ibid., p.* 63.

twelve winds blowing from twelve points of the compass and to recall that ancient maps conventionally represented winds as issuing from a small human head with its puffed-out cheeks blowing furiously. When he realizes further that cherubs are often depicted in old religious pictures as bodiless heads, and that, as shown on a flat map, the winds would describe triangles, he has interpreted the symbol. If he subsequently happens on the following passage in one of Thomas's prose stories, his interpretation is confirmed: "He traced [on the map] with his fingers the lightly drawn triangles of two winds, and the mouths of two cornered cherubs. . . . The cherubs blew harder; wind . . . drove on and on." [8] The symbol has nothing to do with Freud or Jung or whomever; it is taken from cartographic and iconographic convention.

Indeed, the symbolism of Thomas is drawn from a whole variety of sources. It falls under three general heads: (1) natural, (2) conventional, and (3) private. The natural symbolism is of the sort that almost any poet, indeed almost any human being, is likely to employ. Light is a symbol of good or knowledge, dark of evil or ignorance, warmth of life or comfort, cold of death or discomfort, ascent of progress or resurrection, descent of regression or death, and so on. Here, if anywhere, ready-made symbologies might have some force; even so, there is nothing invariable about these symbols in Thomas, nor are they always symbols. Surely there are such *things* as light, dark, warmth, cold, ascent, and descent!

The conventional symbols depend for interpretation upon knowledge of the conventions of the subject from which they are taken. How numerous the kinds of these may be seen from the fact that Thomas draws them from cartography, astronomy and the history of astronomy, physics, chemistry, botany, anatomy, mechanics, and in particular such pseudo-sciences as go under the name *occulta*— astrology, alchemy, witchcraft, and black magic, among others; from games and sports; from a mass of myth and legend, including some rather recondite rabbinical materials; as well as from the more usual resources of literature and history.

The private symbolism can best be interpreted by following him from work to work, whether of verse or prose, and observing his habits. One observes, thus, that he tends to use wax as a symbol of dead or mortal flesh, oil as a symbol of life, the sea as a symbol of the

[8] "The Map of Love," in *The Map of Love: Verse and Prose* (London: J. M. Dent & Sons, Ltd., 1939), p. 64.

source of life, salt as a symbol of genesis in the sea. Scissors or knives are symbols of birth (on the ground that the birth-caul is cut open, the birth-string cut) or of death (on the ground that the thread of life is cut, the branch lopped) and of sexual connection (on the ground of its relation to life and death). He analogizes the anatomy of man to the structure of the universe, too, and sees the human microcosm as an image of the macrocosm, and conversely; and this analogy begets a whole series of symbols. Wounds, one of his most persistent symbols, stand for a number of things: the pain of life, the heart, the navel wound, the sexual parts and the sexual act, Christ, the effects of Time. Tailors are often symbols of what sews man together or sews his shroud or cuts the vital thread. Embalment, particularly of the Egyptian sort, is a symbol of an obstacle that cannot be overcome, or that can be overcome, in the attempt to resurrect the spirit. In all these private symbols there is undoubtedly a fertile field for psychological inquiry; but the psychologist who wishes to investigate had better be willing, first of all, to find out what Thomas is saying.

But why, the reader may very naturally ask at this point, should Thomas have couched his poetry in symbols so esoteric? Indeed, why should he have used symbols at all? Isn't all this a mere riddling and obscuration? Is it necessary for poetry to be as complex as all that? Does this do anything more than complicate the task of reading?

T. S. Eliot has remarked that this age is a complicated one and therefore requires a poetry which is complicated. I am perfectly willing to let this answer content anyone who can be content with it; but I must admit that I do not see the evidence that our age is more complicated than any other, except on a very foreshortened and simplified view of history, and I am not clear in any case why the complexity of an age should necessitate complexity in poetry. (I should like, by the way, the caveman's view on whether lighting a fire is more complex if one rubs sticks or if one presses a button; Spinoza's, let us say, as to whether philosophy is more complex at present than it was in his day; and so on.)

A second notion, much knocked about in the press of late, that contemporary poets have gone in for obscurantism out of sheer perversity, seems even more trivial. I suspect that no answer which depends on what poetry in general *has* to be, in any given age or out of all relation to time, is worth much. Poetry in general does not *have* to be anything determinate at all, as ought to be clear to any-one aware of the vast variety of good poetry in different forms con-trived upon different principles and involving different subjects and devices.

Symbolism itself is merely a device,[9] and a special order of sym-bolism is merely a special order of device; and there is obviously no necessity that poetry or any other art should employ any one device invariably. Thomas is a symbolist, but not all of his poems are sym-bolistic; indeed, as he developed he seems to have drawn farther and farther away from the use of symbolism. A device may be well or ill used; whether it is well or ill used depends upon the powers of the device—what the device can do—and upon its being more or less effective than any other device in meeting the particular exigencies of the individual poem.

Since all the arts involve invention, and continually discover new devices or new uses for old devices, it is never possible to make a list exhaustive of all the possible uses of a given device; but we may note that symbolism has several principal powers. First, since sym-bolism involves the representation of one idea through the medium of another, it can cause us to entertain ideas remote from, or totally outside of, ordinary experience, by the extension of ideas we al-ready possess; thus mystics tend to use symbols in their descriptions of the mystical experience precisely because that experience is an extraordinary one.

Second, since the symbolic concept, the idea which stands for another, is always presented in the form of an image (something which can be either perceived by our senses or imagined), symbols can make immediate and vivid what otherwise would be remote and faint, and thus act powerfully upon our thoughts and emotions. Anyone who has observed the influence of patriotic and religious symbols will be well aware of this particular power of symbolism. Again, symbols can either focus our attention upon a single as-

[9] For a discussion of symbolism as it is conceived in this volume see my "Dia-logue on Symbolism," in Ronald S. Crane, ed., *Critics and Criticism* (Chicago: University of Chicago Press, 1952), esp. pp. 581-87. A much broader and fuller treatment of the subject can be found in Richard P. McKeon's brilliant essay, "Symbols, Myths, and Arguments," originally delivered as a paper at the Thir-teenth Conference on Science, Philosophy, and Religion and published in Lyman Bryson *et al.*, ed., *Symbols and Values: An Initial Study* (New York: Harper & Bros., 1954).

pect of something or cause us to conceive that thing in many aspects simultaneously, and so determine our emotional reactions to it. Death, for example, can be conceived in its benignant or its malignant aspects or both, and produces different emotions as it is differently conceived. The artist who symbolizes it by a smiling shadowy angel presents to us a quite different conceptual aspect, and arouses in us quite different emotions, from those produced by the artist who takes for his symbol the corpse amid all the terrors of the charnel-house. Furthermore, it is possible by the choice of a particular symbol to regulate the degree, as well as determine the kind, of emotional reaction; the artist may, for instance, not only arouse a fear of death by his symbol but arouse greater or less fear by the choice of a symbol more or less dreadful. Finally, we can frequently infer from a given symbol something of the character, beliefs, state of mind, or situation of the person who employed the symbol; we should have little difficulty in inferring, from their different symbols for death, a difference between the pagan Greek and the medieval Christian views of death; and a writer can utilize our tendency to make inferences of this kind, depicting the mood, thought, and character of his personages by letting us see the symbolic processes of their minds.

Other devices—metaphor and simile, particularly—share in these powers; but symbols tend to have much greater range and power. A figure of speech is a figure of speech; whatever it puts before us we tend to contemplate, not as an actuality, but as a manner of speaking. A symbol, on the contrary, exhibits something to us as an actuality, and so affects us more strongly. Metaphor and simile are based upon resemblance only; symbols are based upon many other relations. Tools, instruments, and other agencies often symbolize the art, craft, or process in which they are involved, as pestle and mortar stand for the pharmacist's trade. The product or result may be used, as when the art of the engineer is symbolized by a bastion. Materials or parts, particularly distinctive materials or principal parts, may symbolize the whole produced from them, as when the keystone symbolizes the arch. In all these cases there is no question of resemblance. The cross, for example, is a symbol of Christ, not because it resembled him, but because it was the instrument of his martyrdom and because his martyrdom was the instrument of Christian salvation. Precisely because symbolism rests upon many possible relations, it offers greater difficulty of interpretation, when the symbolic basis is obscure, than metaphor, simile, and other forms of comparison. The latter can be solved by considering what resemblance they are founded on; the interpretation of an obscure symbol is much more complex.

Thomas's, or any poet's, use of symbols must be judged in terms of its effectiveness in the individual poem; but his general tendency to use them is accounted for, in part at least, by the quality of his imagination. He has been praised as a poet who dealt with the "major themes" of birth, life, love, and death; but some of the worst poetry in existence has been written on these themes, and there is nothing inherent in them, as themes, which demands any particular poetic treatment, symbolic or otherwise. What is much more to the point, and what is likely to strike his reader first of all, is Thomas's extraordinary imaginative *conception* of these themes. His imagination permits him to enter into areas of experience previously unexplored or to unveil new aspects of perfectly common experiences. Part, indeed, of his obscurity results from the sheer unfamiliarity of the world which he presents to us; like certain mystics, he is often forced into symbol and metaphor simply because there is no familiar way of expressing something in itself so unfamiliar.

His imagination is first of all a strange one, an odd one; he sees things quite differently from the way in which we should. We should see flowers on a grave; he sees the dead "who periscope through flowers to the sky." [10] We should see the towering flames after a fire raid; he sees "the fire-dwarfed street." [11] We should see geese high in the air; he sees "geese nearly in heaven." [12] He looks into what we should find opaque, looks down at something we are wont to look up at, looks up where we should look down, peers in where we should peer out, and out where we should look in.

His poetic imagination has its limits, but within those it has enormous range and power—so enormous that we are apt to think of it as unlimited. It transports him instantly into the mysteries of the womb; it informs him how the child feels at the moment of birth, how the fetus feels during its process of development, how the seed feels at the moment of conception, how all would feel and think if they were prescient of the whole of life. Death is no terminus for him; he descends into the grave and suffers the strange and secret

[10] *Collected Poems,* p. 5.
[11] *Ibid.,* p. 144.
[12] *Ibid.,* p. xv.

existence of the dead, suffers the resolution of the body into its elements and the transmutation of those elements into other forms of life. He can look back on life as only a dead man could, and can rise from the grave in the Resurrection. The Creation and the ultimate Catastrophe are not limits to him; he penetrates into the mind of God before the Creation, and can feel what would be felt by the scattered particles of a universe utterly dissolved. He can be mineral, vegetable, or beast as easily as he can be man; he can penetrate the depths of the earth and the abysses of the sea, and move about in the depths of the unconscious mind as a diver might walk the ocean bottom.

Here, for example, is the Creation:

> In the beginning was the mounting fire
> That set alight the weathers from a spark,
> A three-eyed, red-eyed spark, blunt as a flower;
> Life rose and spouted from the rolling seas,
> Burst in the roots, pumped from the earth and rock
> The secret oils that drive the grass.[13]

Here is the fetus in the womb:

> In the groin of the natural doorway I crouched
> like a tailor
> Sewing a shroud for a journey . . .[14]

Here is the child at the moment of birth:

> . . . I rush in a crouch the ghost with a hammer, air, . . .[15]

Here is the mysterious interior geography of the body:

> Dawn breaks behind the eyes;
> From poles of skull and toe the windy blood
> Slides like a sea; . . . [16]

Here we are in the world of the other-than-man:

> My images stalk the trees and the slant sap's tunnel,
> No tread more perilous, the green steps and spire
> Mount on man's footfall,
> I with the wooden insect in the tree of nettles,

[13] *Ibid.*, p. 27.
[14] *Ibid.*, p. 110.
[15] *Ibid.*, p. 108.
[16] *Ibid.*, p. 29.

In the glass bed of grapes with snail and flower,
Hearing the weather fall.[17]

Here is one aspect of death:

All issue armoured, of the grave,
The redhaired cancer still alive,
The cataracted eyes that filmed their cloth;
Some dead undid their bushy jaws,
And bags of blood let out their flies; . . .[18]

Here the Resurrection:

. . . I shall waken
To the judge blown bedlam
Of the uncaged sea bottom
The cloud climb of the exhaling tomb
And the bidden dust upsailing
With his flame in every grain.[19]

These are tokens of a mighty, an appalling imagination that sweeps us up with it, like an angel, and forces us to endure the visions of another world, thronged with enchantments and horrors. This is a great natural force, we cannot be unmoved by it; but there is more than natural genius, there is art; we should not stand so in the immediate presence of strange things, did not Thomas exert every power of image, symbol, and metaphor to transport us there. I have said that the use of a particular device must be judged according to what the device can do in a particular context; we can see something of Thomas's use of symbols, and thereby something of the justification of his symbolic method, by examining an instance of it.

Suppose we take as an example a line from the sonnet quoted at the very beginning of this essay. "Abaddon in the hangnail cracked from Adam." The line means that death and perdition were implicit in the flesh since Adam begot it (Abaddon is the Destroying Angel, Death, Apollyon, the Angel of the Bottomless Pit). A literal statement of the sort I have just made, in interpreting the line, is abstract and produces no particular emotion; one turns it over in one's mind, assents or dissents, and dismisses it. A figure of comparison, such as "Death is implicit in the flesh as if the Destroying An-

[17] *Ibid.*, p. 41.
[18] *Ibid.*, p. 4.
[19] *Ibid.*, p. 158.

gel himself dwelt in it," would still emphasize the abstraction, and leave the presence of Abaddon as a merely contemplated possibility, something clearly contrary to fact. But the use of the symbol Abaddon (the only symbol in the line, by the way) confronts us immediately, as a matter of horrid fact, with the Destroying Angel lurking as a physical presence within the mortal flesh, and the mortal flesh is his Bottomless Pit; the flesh which the metaphor "hangnail" makes, not the fruit of Adam's loin, but the merest fragment of his flesh, not much alive when torn from him and incapable of further life on its own. (There is a kind of sublimity of the derisive here; for this poet the flesh of all humanity since Adam is nothing but a hangnail.)

Thomas employs symbols in many ways, but here we see his principal use of them: to make immediate and factual what metaphor and analogue would have left remote and fanciful, to coerce the imagination and so coerce belief; he arouses our emotions before we have time to doubt. Through the repeated use of symbols in this fashion, he builds in his first two volumes, as very real indeed, a fantastic universe of his own.

It is a weird and terrible one. Babes, prescient of the agonies of life and death, speak from the womb or, sitting amid its veils and shadows, paint night and day upon its sides. Men brood on maggots which consume their living flesh as they watch. Flesh grows transparent to reveal the winding nerves and veins and the hidden galleries of bones, the worm gnawing at all. Life struggles out of strange seas and disappears into them, or dissolves to dust. The dead, visible in their tombs, display their corrupting limbs, or spy secretly on the living, or rise to seduce dreaming men. The earth is compact of the debris of the charnel; the landscape hints, in its contours, that it is itself a gigantic corpse. Such love as there is, is preparation for horror or is mere addiction; the flesh falls from the beloved to reveal a mummified corpse, the lover knows himself maddened by the devil's-drug of love. There are greater terrors: women with bagpipe breasts, wounded and mutilated men, men in the forms of plants, animals, and burning candles; a giant runner in the form of a grave, who overtakes all who flee him; a mysterious and sinister scissorman and tailor; scissors that stalk about; ships with shrouds for sails; ghosts, who, manacled to the living man, control his actions from subterranean regions; Cadaver, the one corpse hidden in all flesh, who wears living men as his masks; the grave, in the form of a mon-

strous boxer, whole countries for his hands, who batters men into
the tomb; a strange procession of biblical figures, subtly made sinister; serpents, mandrakes, witches, demons, vampires, nameless animals. There are changing weathers and lights in this world, but for
the most part there is darkness and gloom, lit only occasionally by
dying planets, baleful eyes, or the phosphorescent corruption of the
tomb. It is a nightmare universe, a universe of darkness and fright,
a world under the "forever falling night" of Time; a world unsaved
by Christ, and unsaveable, doomed.

This is the theater of Thomas's early poetry; the reader may ask:
Is it not a Grand Guignol theater? Is this not all stage-magic and
melodrama?

I think we must distinguish between melodrama and tragedy. It
is essential to melodrama, as to the sentimental, romantic, and similar sensational forms,[20] that we should react to the events as events
simply, not as events happening to particularized characters. Thus
we have, in all such kinds, generalized or "stock" characters who,
viewed in terms of their function, are mere circumstances invented
to increase the horror, glamor, or pathos already inherent in the
event. The plucking-out of eyes, for instance, is horrible, no matter
how it happens; it is more horrible if it happens at the hands of a
madman; still more horrible if the madman is a gentle soul who
fancies he is doing it out of kindness; more horrible still if the act
is committed upon an innocent, beautiful, and defenseless girl: such
is the genesis of Grand Guignol characters. Not so in tragedy: the
tragic figure does not take his character from the event; the event
takes on its character from its happening to the tragic figure. When
Oedipus plucks out his eyes, the act is a mere token of the fearful
grief which has already seized on his soul; we react to the self-muti-
lation, not as happening to anyone, or to a particular stock figure,
but as happening to a man of the stature of Oedipus. In sensational
forms character is at a minimum precisely because the emphasis is
upon the events; in tragedy character is maximal because not all
characters are capable of tragic suffering. The characters of a sensational work have no pre-eminence except in suffering, and except
in their suffering are without interest; while the characters of
tragedy have no particular pre-eminence in suffering. Countless

---

[20] I intend by the terms "sentimental" and "romantic," in this passage, the
debased or sensational kinds; for example, the cheaply pathetic soap opera and
the ordinary magazine love story.

thousands have suffered more at the hands of their families than Lear, have had more on their consciences than Macbeth, have got into worse jams than Hamlet. The tragic figure is pre-eminent precisely because of his ethical character and because of its consequence for the way in which he suffers.

Moreover, sensational forms have for their end a sensation merely; tragedy arouses the sensation to produce a more complex reaction. In the melodrama, though we fear the event, we want to be there to witness it, and we want it as gory as possible; in tragedy, we suffer with the protagonist, and we desire the tragic catastrophe, in the end, because it is the only way out which is in keeping with his character. There can be no melodrama if we value the characters highly; there can be no tragedy if we do not. Melodrama of the Grand Guignol kind depends upon, and fosters, our taste for the horrible in itself; tragedy, even the kind written by Webster and Tourneur, employs the horrible only because of its relation to a serious view of life.

Doubtless Thomas, like Baudelaire, is at times nothing more than a stage-musician and frights us with fires patently false. But it is naïve to suppose, as Shaw does in his criticism of Shakespeare, that because poetry involves touches that might be effective in melodrama, it is itself melodramatic. The essence of the sensational forms is that they exaggerate and readily depart from truth in order to achieve the sensation they propose; the essence of tragedy is that its action must embody grave and universal truths. The world of the early Thomas is not a melodramatic one because, as symbolic, it presupposes a reference of its horrors to something further, and does not propose them for their own sake; it does not exaggerate, it can barely approximate, the horror of what it symbolizes. Thomas tells us that to a serious and sensitive individual, life in the absence of a sustaining faith is a nightmare, and so it is; that it is the worst of nightmares, and it is; and if that nightmare is as horrible as possible, images which adumbrate that horror do not exaggerate it— they express it. Without their reference, the symbols of Thomas would be melodramatic, even morbid; because they have reference to the serious suffering of a man of some nobility, they are tragic.

"There was a Saviour"

by Winifred Nowottny

In this study of Dylan Thomas's "There was a Saviour," I hope to show how the peculiarity of the language compels us to set about constructing a meaning for it, and how it is that the poem contrives to direct us towards the particular kind of meaning that must be apprehended in order to make sense of the language of the poem.

THERE WAS A SAVIOUR

> There was a saviour
> Rarer than radium,
> Commoner than water, crueller than truth;
> Children kept from the sun
> Assembled at his tongue
> To hear the golden note turn in a groove,
> Prisoners of wishes locked their eyes
> In the jails and studies of his keyless smiles.
>
> The voice of children says
> From a lost wilderness
> There was calm to be done in his safe unrest,
> When hindering man hurt
> Man, animal, or bird
> We hid our fears in that murdering breath,
> Silence, silence to do, when earth grew loud,
> In lairs and asylums of the tremendous shout.
>
> There was glory to hear
> In the churches of his tears,
> Under his downy arm you sighed as he struck,

O you who could not cry
On to the ground when a man died
Put a tear for joy in the unearthly flood
And laid your cheek against a cloud-formed shell:
Now in the dark there is only yourself and myself.

Two proud, blacked brothers cry,
Winter-locked side by side,
To this inhospitable hollow year,
O we who could not stir
One lean sigh when we heard
Greed on man beating near and fire neighbour
But wailed and nested in the sky-blue wall
Now break a giant tear for the little known fall,

For the drooping of homes
That did not nurse our bones,
Brave deaths of only ones but never found,
Now see, alone in us,
Our own true strangers' dust
Ride through the doors of our unentered house.
Exiled in us we arouse the soft,
Unclenched, armless, silk and rough love that breaks all
    rocks.

Dylan Thomas himself, in a broadcast reading of some of his
poems, described this poem as being among those of his "that do
move a little way towards the state and destination I imagine I intended to be theirs when, in small rooms in Wales, arrogantly and
devotedly I began them." [1] There is then, to sustain us through the
difficulties of understanding the poem, some warrant that the poet
himself thought that it had been worthwhile to write it.

The poem does indeed present considerable difficulty. Even the
syntax is difficult. The immediately striking thing about the syntax
is the peculiarity of the tenses and pronouns.[2] In reading the poem

---

[1] *Quite Early One Morning: Broadcasts by Dylan Thomas* (4th printing; London: J. M. Dent and Sons, Ltd., 1954), p. 130.
[2] Readers apprehensive of seeing the poem reduced to a grammatical exercise
may perhaps feel less suspicious if they note that there is reason to suppose
that Dylan Thomas himself thought that tense has some importance to poetry.
Speaking of three poems of his which, he said, "will, one day, form separate
parts of a long poem which is in preparation," he remarked, "The remembered
tellings, which are the components of the poem, are not all told as though they
are remembered; the poem will not be a series of poems in the past tense. The
memory, in all tenses, can look towards the future, can caution and admonish.

it is difficult to make out, at first, what point in time we are supposed to be looking at or looking from. It begins in an unplaced
past: "There was." In stanza 2 this unplaced past becomes even less
easy to locate, since it becomes part of something told by "The voice
of children . . . From a lost wilderness." Now that T. S. Eliot's
work is so prominent a part of the modern reader's experience of
poetry, we are all rather cautious about the voices of children coming from such places as rose gardens or wildernesses; we know by
now that these are unlikely to be embodied voices, and are more
likely to be figments or haunters or intimations of something lost,
buried in the past, or unattainable. In the course of stanza 3 the
poem moves into the present: "Now . . . there is only yourself and
myself." The fourth stanza, from the vantage-point of the present,
speaks again about the past. The fifth stanza speaks in a kind of
eternal Now, even a prophetic Now: "we arouse the . . . love that
breaks all rocks."

The pronouns shift too. The change in the pronouns is very
striking at the words (stanza 3), "O you who could not cry" (this is
the first appearance of "you") and again (stanza 4) when this form
of words is almost repeated but the pronoun changes back to "we":
"O we who could not stir." It would be a reasonable inference from
this series of changes that "we" and "you" are somehow the same
and yet somehow different. If, struck by these changes, we ask what
exactly is done with the pronouns from first to last, we find that
stanza 1 speaks of "saviour" and "children" and uses the pronouns
"his" and "their," in stanza 2 the situation is that "we" did this and
that in "his . . . unrest," in stanza 3 "his" persists but "we" is replaced by "you"—in three different uses at that, as may be seen by
considering them one by one. The first use of "you" is in "you
sighed as he struck" (stanza 3). It is most natural to take this as the
generalizing use, equivalent to "everybody," a use implying "anybody in the same situation would feel the same"; "you" is often used
in this way to introduce a description of a common and familiar
reaction. The same stanza's second use of "you" is in "O you who
could not." Here the pronoun is the opposite of universalizing. To
say "O you . . ." to anyone is normally to mean *you as distinct from
me, you who are different from me.* The stanza's third use is in

---

The rememberer may live himself back into active participation in the remembered scene, adventure, or spiritual condition." (See *Quite Early One Morning*,
pp. 155, 157.)

"only yourself and myself." The poet doesn't say "only us," or "only you and I"; he says something radically ambiguous, for "only yourself and myself" could be intimate (*only the two of us, together*) or it could be separative (distinguishing *your self* from *my self*). The people referred to in this phrase may be very intimately together, or on the other hand it may be (or may at the same time be) that their confrontation is startling. It may even be that each one of them is, as we sometimes say, alone with himself. This obscure situation becomes even more puzzling when we realize that the syntax of the lines containing these changes is continuous: from "O you" to "yourself and myself" there is no break. (Moreover the "yourself and myself" become in the ensuing stanzas "we" again—looking back to the "We" of stanza 2, which itself looks back to "children" in stanza 1.) It would seem, then, that it is being forced upon our notice that this is a poem about continuous identities with a changing outlook, taken at various points in a continuum running through the poem. The poem starts with a number of children who all feel or are taught to feel the same about a saviour; then in stanza 2 the children recede into the past, where only their voice remains, telling—as from a distance—more about experiences of the saviour and of attitudes to him and to the world; in stanza 3 a speaker (unidentified) generalizes about everybody's attitude to the saviour, then makes a distinction between that attitude and some other; then speaks suddenly from the darkness of "Now" in which there is "only yourself and myself"; if only these, then presumably no saviour. Of course, what brings about the change of pronouns in stanza 3 is the vanishing of the saviour out of the picture: whereas formerly there was a collective attitude to him, now two identities detach themselves from this shared attitude and have a real encounter, in which—as stanzas 4 and 5 show—they feel really one with each other and talk of themselves in a new sense as "we": we who now have compassion. As this new "we," these "two brothers" now have the attributes of the saviour. (Perhaps one should, more precisely, say that they have attributes commonly associated with the concept "saviour.") Now they look back at the living and address them with a message that takes the form of a revaluation of their own lives on earth and a proclamation of the power of love.

Thus the tenses and pronouns carry the most important thing in the structure of the poem: that is, the fundamental process of the poem, its beginning with children taught about a saviour and its

moving on through their lives to death and the redefinition of salvation. All the contrasts in the diction of the poem hang upon, or
are related to, the process expressed through the changing pronouns
and tenses.

But the contrasts in the diction are far from simple. Even a cur-
sory look at the diction of stanzas 1-3 is enough to make one realize
that the question of what those old values were, which the brothers' values replace, can have no simple, immediate answer. The
diction of stanzas 1-3 is violently difficult in its repeated use of oxy-
moron (e.g., "locked their eyes In . . . keyless smiles," "safe unrest"), in its indeterminacy as to whether the saviour and his devotees are good or bad, and above all in its strangeness of a kind
R. N. Maud describes well when he says, "Reading Dylan Thomas,
we rarely find uncommon words; yet all the words seem tantaliz-
ingly unfamiliar, pressed by the poet into strange image-combinations." [3] Since the diction is so baffling, it may be as well to find out
first whether there are any clear patterns in the ground-plan of the
poem or in its verbal devices; the poem does not adhere to the
idiom of common life, so there is no way open to us but to find
out whether it has an expressiveness of its own, in its own terms.

Looking at the general plan of the poem, one observes first that
the poem seems to turn on a hinge in the line, "Now in the dark
there is only yourself and myself." The word "Now," with which
this hinge-line begins, is also used to begin two other lines in the
poem, which may suggest to us that these lines, like that, act as
nodal points in the system of contrasts or series of developments
running through the poem and underlying the peculiarities of the
diction. And so in fact it proves. In the line "Now see, alone in
us, . . ." (stanza 5) the word "see" looks back through the poem to
"in the dark," and "alone in us" looks back to "only yourself and
myself." The other "Now . . ." line, "Now break a giant tear for the
little known fall," goes back to "O you who could not cry" and to
"Put a tear for joy" in stanza 3 and to "O you who could not stir
One lean sigh" and "wailed" in its own stanza (4). Moreover this
"Now . . ." of stanza 4 is very emphatically signalled as some kind
of new departure by a change in the rhyme-scheme and the linea-
tion: it is here that the only full rhyme in the poem ("wall"/"fall")
occurs, and this is the only line to occupy the end-position in a
stanza and yet not to stand aligned with the one before (all the

[3] In "Dylan Thomas's Poetry," *Essays in Criticism,* IV (1954), 416.

other stanzas end with a pair of lines printed as one prints a couplet, but stanza 4's penultimate line is indented as a "short" line). Everything possible is done to emphasize that at the word "Now" a new development takes place and a new stage in the argument of the poem gets under way.

If "Now"-lines introduce changes, we must ask ourselves what marked change occurs along with the third of these, "Now see, alone in us" [stanza 5]: that is, we must ask what is new about the last five lines of the poem, what aspect of the world of the poem they set in a new light. The most obvious answer to such a question would seem to be that in this part of the poem the brothers' attitude or message ceases to be merely, or generally, something to do with compassion; the poem now moves on instead into the terminology and imagery of sexual love between man and woman. The problem for the reader is to know what to make of this, since it is far from being made immediately evident what relation obtains between the triumphant sexuality ("Ride through the doors of our unentered house") and universal liberation ("breaks all rocks") of these lines, and the concerns of the preceding stanzas. We can, however, say that the ground-plan of the poem has the outstanding characteristic that there are three hinges or turns in the argument, and that the first turn has to do with the vanishing of the saviour, the second turn has to do with expression of human compassion, and the third has to do with the entry of sexual love. We may then suppose that these themes, if we may call them so, must be related to the peculiarities of the diction.

To make this supposition does not instantly result in a clarification of the peculiar expressions the poet uses; the diction does not so easily declare the logic of its mysteries. It is almost as though the poet had gone out of his way to write a kind of language that is "symbolist" in the sense Wallace Stevens expresses so well when he writes in the opening lines of his poem "Man Carrying Thing":

> The poem must resist the intelligence
> Almost successfully. Illustration:
>
> A brune figure in winter evening resists
> Identity. The thing he carries resists
>
> The most necessitous sense . . .[4]

[4] *The Collected Poems of Wallace Stevens* (London: Faber and Faber, Ltd., 1959), p. 350.

If we ask what the point is in writing of this kind, perhaps the answer is at hand in the conclusion of this same poem by Stevens:

> We must endure our thoughts all night, until
> The bright obvious stands motionless in cold.

If there is indeed a "bright obvious" to be reached for, through the struggle to understand why the poet has chosen just these (baffling) expressions, it seems likely that we shall not get at it unless we look for what the diction can tell us about itself through characteristics that recur with sufficient frequency and emphasis to suggest that some pressure of meaning has extruded these curious forms; we must look, that is to say, for striking formal relations at the level of the diction.

To readers who are familiar with the symbolism of William Blake, one aspect of the imagery of the poem will stand out very sharply: its preoccupation with buildings and rocks. In the symbolism of Blake, rock or stone, and buildings made of these, are associated with evil, as being manifestations of the forces that produce the dark Satanic mills, the modern industrial hell, the obscurantism of institutionalized religion, tyranny and war. Dylan Thomas's poem too uses images of rock and of building ("jails and studies," "churches," "wall," "rocks"). But even without knowledge of Blake, one might grasp (since it is prominent both by its peculiarity and by its repetition) the importance of the formal relationship between

> In the jails and studies of his keyless smiles
> In   lairs and asylums of the tremendous shout
> In the churches   of his tears

where the sense of the poem declares itself through a persistent verbal pattern suggesting persistent analogy. The constant elements in the pattern are:

> In the *buildings* of   [*some expression of*] *human feeling*

and if we go back to what precedes the "In," and ask *what* is "in" these buildings, we find another contant element, for what is in them is again something to do with human beings:

> locked their eyes/In
> silence to do, . . ./In
> glory to hear/In

The abstractable common pattern is:

something human   in the buildings of   something human.

The term that sticks out as not belonging is always the building-term. The "we" of the poem and the "saviour" of the poem are presented in human terms but between them there intervene buildings. This is a very peculiar pattern, but its very peculiarity and its repetitiveness give it a prominence that attracts our attention, and, moreover, we are not left without the necessary directive for interpreting it. The directive is most sustainedly given in the first stanza. There, on the first appearance of the pattern, in "Prisoners of wishes locked their eyes In the jails and studies of his keyless smiles," the "smiles" are explicitly described as "keyless," and we are explicitly told that those who contrive to lock eyes in the jails and studies of these smiles are themselves the prisoners not of the smiles but of wishes; that is to say, it is because they are prisoners *of wishes* that they *transform* the smiles of the saviour into jails.

R. N. Maud has said of Dylan Thomas's "strange image-combinations" that "the first step in overcoming the strangeness is to insist to ourselves that the poem means literally what it says." [5] No doubt it is true that people who are familiar with the idiom of Dylan Thomas tend to use the word "literally" in a sense peculiar to the context of their experience of getting at Thomas's meaning. Elder Olson puts the difficulty clearly: "What did a poet, so obviously given to metaphor and symbol in his poetry, mean by saying that he wanted to be read literally?" [6] It is true that Dylan Thomas himself said he wanted his words to be taken "literally," and indeed, a propos of a phrase in the very poem with which we are now concerned, he wrote to Vernon Watkins,

I'm so glad you liked my lyrical poem, that you thought it was one of my best. I'll think of "stupid kindred," which is right, of course, in meaning and which prevents any ambiguity, but kindred seems a little pompous a word: it hasn't the literal simplicity of hindering man.[7]

[5] In *Essays in Criticism,* IV (1964), 416.
[6] Elder Olson, *The Poetry of Dylan Thomas* (Chicago: University of Chicago Press, 1954), p. 61.
[7] *Dylan Thomas, Letters to Vernon Watkins* (London: J. M. Dent and Sons and Faber and Faber, Ltd. 1957), p. 81. From another passage, in a postscript to the same letter ("To avoid ambiguity, and also the use of the word 'kindred' I've turned 'his' in line 6 of verse 2 into 'that.'") it is clear that the ambiguity to be avoided was the possibility of relating "his breath" to "hindering man."

This passage shows that whatever "literal simplicity" meant exactly, it certainly meant something opposed to being "a little pompous." This would seem to suggest that "literal," for Thomas, is not opposed to "figurative" or to "metaphorical" but rather to techniques of expressing meaning by depending on the meanings words acquire from the sort of situation in which they are usually chosen (in preference to other words having reference to the same thing, but not having the same overtone of attitude to that thing). It seems to me that if we are to take Dylan Thomas "literally," what we are required to do is to interpret his language (in this respect) rather as one interprets the language of a child. The child uses the phrase that seems to him to be the most direct and accurate description of what he is talking about, but because adult conventions of meaning demand that we say what we mean in the way other people would say it, the child's description strikes us, not as factual, but as quaint or even incomprehensible. It is, I think, because of some such characteristic of the style, that though Dylan Thomas means exactly what he says, it is still difficult to identify what is being described—if we persist in expecting to have things described according to common stereotypes of description. I take it, then, that in the phrase "prisoners of wishes" what is meant is that "wishes" are prisons to the people who cannot break free of them and who, therefore, are "kept from the sun" (or, since stanza 1 allows of this construction, keep children from the sun). The obverse side of Thomas's "literal" technique is that though he uses words with almost childish directness, and "innocence" of the proprieties of usage, their "factual" reference is often to the "facts" that only the sophisticated adult would know about. It is at this point that, in order to understand Thomas's language, one has to look before one leaps. The necessary leap, here, is to the Freudian interpretation of the psyche. (That is also, in a sense sufficiently approximate, Blake's view of the psyche.) In that interpretation, people who have repressed their desires are always so busy repressing them that they cut themselves off from life as it might naturally be (cf. "kept from the sun"). The "prisoners of wishes" then are people suffering from repressions, who connect this process (arbitrarily) with the smiles of the saviour; there is no real connection between the repressions and the saviour's smiles; it is the repressed themselves who set up the connection and make the saviour's smiles into jails. "Keyless," again, is "literal" in this peculiar double sense. In the direct way of the child, it observes that smiles have no keys. But there is also a leap to be made to a situation in which a saviour would, to the knowledgeable mind, have a connection with keys. The necessary leap is to St. Peter, to whom Christ said (Matthew, xvi, 18-19), "Thou art Peter, and upon this rock I will build my church; and the gates of hell shall not prevail against it. And I will give unto thee the keys of the kingdom of heaven." (The problem of how one is to know which way to jump, to arrive at the right area of knowledge and associations and so to see a "literal" or "factual" meaning in these imagistic descriptions, is one that will recur in a much more acute form, when some literary allusions are discussed, later on in this commentary.[8] Here it is perhaps sufficient to observe that St Peter's connection with rock, and the prevalence of rock-references in the poem, and its concern with "churches," together make this as good a guess as any.)[9] I think it should also be observed that there is also a certain difficulty in relating Thomas's "literal" technique (even if we allow for its reliance on sophisticated "facts") to his other and sometimes concurrent practice of expecting us to catch the reverberations of an expression against the minutely-differentiated various usages of stereotypes analogously related to it; "keyless," for instance, may very well share in that Joycean technique (dear to Thomas) of making one expression a palimpsest of references and travestied usages; it does seem to me that "keyless" gives us an echo-bounce to *clueless,* and if so there is nothing one could call even remotely "literal"

[8] See the note at the end of this essay.
[9] For the thorniness of the problem, cf. M. C. Beardsley's discussion, in his *Aesthetics,* p. 158, of Olson's treatment (p. 74) of Sonnet V of *Altarwise by owl-light:* "It is hard to see what plausible principles would justify the method of explication used by Elder Olsen [*sic*] . . . for example, he says that 'And from the windy West came two-gunned Gabriel' refers to the constellation Perseus, for Perseus had two weapons, his sword and the Medusa's head; two guns recall the Wild West, the West recalls poker, poker is a game of cards, cards suggest trumps, and trumps suggest the Last Trump, hence Gabriel. . . . Is there any limit to explication by this method? See Theodore Spencer, 'How to Criticize a Poem,' *New Republic,* CIX (December 6, 1943), 816-17; but it is a nice question at what point his attack becomes unjust." But cf. also Beardsley, op. cit., p. 145: "A proposed explication may be regarded as a hypothesis that is tested by its capacity to account for the greatest quantity of data in the words of the poem— including their potential connotations—and in most poems for which alternative hypotheses can be offered it will turn out in the end that one is superior to the other."

about this indirect meaning. Again, this interpretation of what "literal" means at the stylistic level does not exclude the further possibility that the style permits also of specific reference to a particular identifiable situation. An interpretation "literal" in this sense would say that the children of stanza 1 are not vaguely in any imprisoning jail or study but are in Sunday-school (as, in stanza 3, somebody is in a church and, later on, in a grave). We are then in the very thorny position that this diction means what it says (though it does not say what it means in the ways other people would do) but it also asks us to make leaps to particular areas of knowledge and terminology, and sometimes it may mean what it doesn't *quite* say (as in "keyless"/[clueless]) and it probably also has reference to a specific situation ultimately identifiable if we can grasp the complicated idiom of the poem.

Despite the difficulties outlined above I think it is fair enough to say that the first stanza does succeed in making it so difficult to get any sense out of it *unless* one takes a leap to the assumptions of modern psychiatric theory, that we can hardly read the poem at all without being conscious that it is going to relate its concerns to what any reaonably sophisticated reader might be expected to know about Freud. (Whether the poet "has a right" to take this knowledge for granted is not my business to argue; I would argue only that the poet does take it for granted.)

In subsequent stanzas the reader is not so explicitly told what stage of psychological development the words refer to. The explicitness of "children" and "Prisoners of wishes" is not kept up in what follows; we are left more to our own devices of placing the speakers of subsequent stanzas in the appropriate position on the Freudian graph. But we are given clues at least adequate to enable us to do this. (If it be complained that the poet is asking rather a lot of us, it might be retorted that he has rather a lot to get in anyway, since—as it now appears—he is concerned not only with the relation of people to a saviour, and to other people, but also with the psychological drive within the people.)

Stanza 2 speaks of "the tremendous shout." This would seem to bring in the cry from the Cross. But what can it mean, on the Freudian graph, to say that the speakers of the poem hid their fears in lairs and asylums of the tremendous shout? It seems reasonable to suppose that this line, following the language-pattern of the last line of the first stanza, must, like that, have a psychological as well as a religious reference in the pattern of its ideas. We may take it, at least, that the psychological phase referred to is one that follows childhood, since in this stanza the children have receded into the past; the presumption, therefore, that this is the phase of adolescence is warranted by the phrase "safe unrest"—which one might say was a factual description of normal adolescence—and by the fact that the stanza makes sense if we refer its language to that stage of development of the psyche in which the dominant concern is a complex relation with the father-figure, the symbol of Authority towards whom the rebellious adolescent has feelings of hate, guilt, fear, and an unconscious expectation, even desire, of punishment. Correspondingly, in religious terms, the saviour becomes the scapegoat (the religious attitude mirroring the emotional attitude). Stanza 3's relation to this train of ideas must be dealt with later, lest in treating it we should at this point have to make its diction bear all the weight of a reading whose corroboration is to be found in aspects of the poem not yet discussed.

Thus in stanzas 1 and 2 something human about the saviour becomes (metaphorically) for his devotees something built of rock or stone and devoted to purposes associated with imprisonment ("jails"), with education or indoctrination ("studies"), and then with fear and ferocity and concealment ("lairs") and madness and refuge ("asylums"). As to these "fears" that were "hid" in "lairs and asylums," we may ask, is the beast in the lair fearful or fearsome? Is the asylum a madhouse or a sanctuary? The metaphor, it would seem, is becoming both ambiguous and ambivalent. It is now much nastier (implying lurking beast and madman) and yet at the same time more pitiful (if we look at the matter from the side of the hunted beast or the insane). The saviour too changes; his progress is from smiles to the tremendous cry from the Cross. What is happening is that the saviour and his devotees are changing together.

In stanza 3 the increasing interpenetration of saviour and believers goes a stage further again: whereas in stanza 2 the believers had recourse to the saviour in fear and mental confusion, in stanza 3 the fear and confusion are replaced by a complacent (and evidently perverted) enjoyment:

> There was glory to hear
> In the churches of his tears,
> Under his downy arm you sighed as he struck,

and here the strained linguistic connection which was so striking in "hid . . . fears in . . . shout" gives place to the less strained connection "glory to hear In the churches." Now the devotees are "Under his downy arm." Now the devotees rejoice—in suffering, it would seem; they "Put a tear for joy in the . . . flood." The people concerned appear to be churchgoers, presumably adults, and the "glory" they are enjoying, if the word has a simply factual, specific ground, may equally well be elaborate church music, a martial hymn, or the "music" of tears; the language is permissive of all these interpretations—they glory in whatever it is that they hear in churches. It is notable, too, that "the churches of his tears" may be taken in one way that is not (if we relate it to other usages) metaphorical at all; one may speak without a metaphor of "the Church of St. Michael and All Angels," this being an accepted way of naming churches and giving them a special dedication. By analogy with that, "churches of his tears" means something like churches *dedicated to* tears; as a metaphor analogous to other members of this metaphor-pattern in the poem, it means that the tears of the saviour have been metamorphosed into an institutionalized church whose members glory in suffering and in whatever else "glory" stands for in the context. Translated into the Freudian scheme, this stanza presumably is a comment on the alleged element of sado-masochism in some religious attitudes and on the alleged element of perversion in the personal emotions of those who find these religious attitudes congenial.

To sum up what we have so far: with the aid of this little language-pattern involving images of buildings, we have found that the cult of the saviour, as presented in the poem, is radically unlike the nature of the saviour himself; man remakes the saviour in his own image by distorting him to correspond with the distorted views and institutions that dominate society; in stanza 1 education is indicted; in stanza 3 the organized church is indicted. What then is indicted in stanza 2? That is to say, what institution or what aspect of organized society is referred to in "lairs and asylums"? I do not see any easy way of answering this question satisfactorily at this point, but it may prove, later on, that other aspects of the poem suggest an acceptable answer. The fourth and fifth stanzas look forward to the cure, the new salvation, described at the end of the poem breaking "all rocks." This cure is not merely brotherly compassion, as in stanza 4, for in stanza 5 it is suggested that the cure ultimately resides at a much deeper level, in the release of sexual love, for it is a sexual love that the brothers see, in the concluding lines, as a liberated and liberating force. This liberation concludes the Freudian pattern in the poem.[10]

[10] Mrs. Nowottny goes on to argue that this pattern should be viewed in relation to a further pattern of literary allusions; that the poem is a critique rather than a rejection of religious attitudes; it concerns the growth of a poet's mind, and its *persona* is that of a poet who "in a time of war examines the religious and cultural symbols that have themselves in great measure shaped the intelligence and feeling that turn to question the meaning of their world."

Last Poems

by Ralph Maud

*"I consider that it is the chief duty of the interpreter to begin
analyses and to leave them unfinished."*

C. S. Lewis, *Allegory of Love*

In examining Dylan Thomas's early poems we must consider
what lies behind their obscurity; with the last poems we have to ask
what lies behind their comparative clarity. The "Note" to the
Collected Poems, dated November 1952, seems especially appli-
cable to the later poems of the volume: they were written "for the
love of Man and in praise of God." But behind that solemnity one
can hear the poet's alternative phrasing to John Malcolm Brinnin
in July 1951: "poems in praise of God's world by a man who doesn't
believe in God." [1] The answer to the riddle posed by these statements is perhaps best sought in the poems themselves, for instance
in "Over Sir John's hill," where universal mortality is symbolized
in the actual scene from the poet's window overlooking the estuary
of the Taf and Towy at Laugharne, South Wales. God is mentioned
twice in the poem; we seek the significance of these two allusions:

> Over Sir John's hill,
> The hawk on fire hangs still;
> In a hoisted cloud, at drop of dusk, he pulls to his claws
> And gallows, up the rays of his eyes the small birds of the bay
> And the shrill child's play
> Wars

[1] John Malcolm Brinnin, *Dylan Thomas in America* (Boston: Little, Brown,
1955), p. 128.

Of the sparrows and such who swansing, dusk, in wrangling hedges.
And blithely they squawk
To fiery tyburn over the wrestle of elms until
The flash the noosed hawk
Crashes, and slowly the fishing holy stalking heron
In the river Towy below bows his tilted headstone.

Flash, and the plumes crack,
And a black cap of jack-
Daws Sir John's just hill dons, and again the gulled birds hare
To the hawk on fire, the halter height, over Towy's fins,
In a whack of wind.
There
Where the elegiac fisherbird stabs and paddles
In the pebbly dab-filled
Shallow and sedge, and "dilly dilly," calls the loft hawk,
"Come and be killed,"
I open the leaves of the water at a passage
Of psalms and shadows among the pincered sandcrabs prancing

And read, in a shell,
Death clear as a buoy's bell:
All praise of the hawk on fire in hawk-eyed dusk be sung,
When his viperish fuse hangs looped with flames under the brand
Wing, and blest shall
Young
Green chickens of the bay and bushes cluck, "dilly dilly,
Come let us die."
We grieve as the blithe birds, never again, leave shingle and elm,
The heron and I,
I young Aesop fabling to the near night by the dingle
Of eels, saint heron hymning in the shell-hung distant

Crystal harbour vale
Where the sea cobbles sail,
And wharves of water where the walls dance and the white cranes stilt.
It is the heron and I, under judging Sir John's elmed
Hill, tell-tale the knelled
Guilt
Of the led-astray birds whom God, for their breast of whistles,
Have mercy on,
God in his whirlwind silence save, who marks the sparrows hail,
For their souls' song.

Now the heron grieves in the weeded verge. Through windows
Of dusk and water I see the tilting whispering

Heron, mirrored, go,
As the snapt feathers snow,
Fishing in the tear of the Towy. Only a hoot owl
Hollows, a grassblade blown in cupped hands, in the looted elms
And no green cocks or hens
Shout
Now on Sir John's hill. The heron, ankling the scaly
Lowlands of the waves,
Makes all the music; and I who hear the tune of the slow,
Wear-willow river, grave,
Before the lunge of the night, the notes on this time-shaken
Stone for the sake of the souls of the slain birds sailing.

Do sparrows have souls? In what theological sense can they possibly be saved? Or, to recast the question in keeping with the para-
ble nature of the poem, do human beings (with their "shrill, child's-
play wars") have immortal souls whose destiny depends on God's
mercy being evoked by prayer? The same kind of question attends
the basic courtroom metaphor in the poem. As often before,
Thomas is acting out a common expression: "We are all condemned to die." In the traditional religious sense we are *condemned*
by Adam's original sin, and are personally *saved* by the redemption
of Christ. The use of "save," "blest," "mercy," etc. in the poem
suggests the traditional approach; but the poem doesn't really go
beyond the mere suggestion. The word "guilt" is used, but without
seriously indicating in what sense the small birds (or we unknown
soldiers) are guilty. Although Sir John's hill puts on the black cap
for our death sentence, there is no real judgment as there is no
real crime. Where a little sermonizing of the scene might be expected in the poem, one looks in vain. The hawk-executioner,
especially, might have been given moral import; but the poet's intention seems to have been quite the opposite.

It is worthwhile looking closely at the language used to describe
the hawk, and this is one case where there is little doubt as to the
kind of decision that produced the particular wording. Harvard
College Library has the working papers for this poem, and although
they are extensive and cumbersome (forty-seven sheets for the single
poem), we can with a high degree of accuracy follow the poet from
the first conception to the completed poem. Some phrases are

worked and reworked up to forty-one times. We are given an opportunity to see exactly what kind of pains Thomas took. Pertinent to our concern with the personality, if any, of the hawk is the phrase "halter height" in the second stanza of the poem:

> . . . and again the gulled birds hare
> To the hawk on fire, the halter height, over Towy's fins.

As we might expect, the words are descriptive and symbolic at the same time. The hawk catches the last rays of the sun and is "on fire"—this is apt description. But it is also symbolic, connected to the doomsday-explosion symbolism running through the poem, by which the hawk is viewed as a gunpowder fuse ready to go off. Thus, the hawk is as much a metaphor for the symbolic fire as the fire is a metaphoric way of describing the hawk. The poet's efforts in the work sheets are directed toward finding the diction that will successfully act this double role, symbolic description and descriptive symbolism.

The "hawk on fire" in the passage above began, it seems, quite simply as the "high hawk." What appears to be the next draft incorporates both the gallows and the gunpowder images in "the hempen firing hawk," a foreshadowing of the final phrase, "the hawk on fire, the halter height." The work sheets often show that first thoughts are the best, but the poet proves it to himself by trying out alternatives. In subsequent rewritings of this part of the poem we find him substituting different phrases while simply recopying the adjacent lines. He introduces a brutal image of slaughter: "the skinning hawk." Then, as though to soften somewhat the picture of tearing flesh, the hawk is abstracted to one aspect of itself, its height above the bay. Thus we have "the skinning height" that the small birds hare to. But "skinning" is subsequently replaced by a reversion to the gallows theme with "the hanging height." Soon "hanging," not quite right, is intensified to "lynching." "The lynching height" appears several times in the drafts while the poet adjusts such phrases as "over the river Towy finned," neatened to "over Towy's fins." Then there is one particular three square inches of a page in which Thomas lists further possibilities —"dusky height," "hempen height," and "hempen caudle height." "Caudle," a sweet drink, is appropriate to the gaiety with which the little victims fly up to their death. But, further, "hempen caudle" has been used by Shakespeare to mean "a hanging," and no doubt

Thomas was thinking of following suit.[2] But neither this nor any of the others seems to have been as satisfactory as "lynching height," which is used as a stand-by until finally crossed out in favor of "halter height" near the end of the work on the poem.

"Halter height" is not the choice that might have appealed to some poets. It is more cold and bloodless than "skinning" and "lynching," for instance. The only explanation for Thomas's passing over these more violent words is that their connotations must have been undesirable. They both imply vindictiveness; whereas "halter" does not. The work sheets show Thomas deliberately finding a neutral adjective for his killer-hawk. He does not want death to appear hateful. As for "hempen," which is neutral enough, it gives perhaps an unwanted notion of texture; the hawk is not a sack but a noose. There was possibly nothing wrong with "hanging height" except commonplaceness. "Halter" says the same thing as "hanging" but more interestingly. "Halter" is also the harness for a driven animal. Besides the point that death is amoral and un-judging, Thomas seems to want to say that mortality is a burden taken on by all. Like the sea of "A Refusal to Mourn the Death, by Fire, of a Child in London," we are all "tumbling in harness"; and the "halter" here signifies the final pull of that harness.

Death is not just (or unjust), Sir John's hill is not judging, the birds are not guilty, the heron is not holy, and God is not, in any meaningful sense, merciful. What, then, are we to think of a poem in which such adjectives are applied to such individuals? Perhaps we should bear in mind, to begin with, that the common expression "condemned to die" does not, when one thinks about it, really mean condemned, *punished* by death. It is just a way of saying "shall or will die"—simple futurity. But there is a rightness about "condemned"; it corresponds to the feeling of grievance against death. The word is not irresponsible; neither, I think, is Thomas. The poem may be expressing only the *fact* of death, and such words as "guilt" may be empty of intellectual content; but a form of meaning is communicated to the emotions, the reader's compassion is guided. One usually frowns on poetry that has vague emotional

[2] "Ye shall have a hempen caudle then, and the help of hatchet"—*Henry VI*, pt. 2, IV. vii. 95. When *OED* records only one other instance of this kind of comic reference to hanging (in the Marprelate Epistles), one is intrigued by the question of where Thomas got the phrase in the first place if not from the *OED* itself. Perhaps he knew his early Shakespeare histories and Marprelate tracts better than one might suppose?

wording without precise denotation. Such a dismissal would not, I think, meet the case here. Thomas should be given credit for expressing truly the chief tenet of the nonreligious: that the intellect cannot handle the fact of death, and that it is sternness, rebellion, hatred, self-pity, compassion—some naked emotion—with which we are left to face the situation. From among these emotions it is Thomas's inclination to choose compassion and to use the words, new or old, which will succeed in expressing it for him.

We get a closer look at the God of "Over Sir John's hill" in a prose note about a projected long poem to be entitled "In Country Heaven," of which that poem along with "In country sleep" and "In the white giant's thigh" would form separate parts. The frame for the pieces is the scene in heaven when God hears of the end of the world:

The godhead, the author, the milky-way farmer, the first cause, architect, lamplighter, quintessence, the beginning Word, the anthropomorphic bowler-out and black-baller, the stuff of all men, scapegoat, martyr, maker, woe-bearer—He, on top of a hill in Heaven, weeps whenever, outside that state of being called his country, one of his worlds drops dead, vanishes screaming, shrivels, explodes, murders itself. And, when He weeps, Light and His tears glide down together, hand in hand. So, at the beginning of the projected poem, He weeps, and Country Heaven is suddenly dark. Bushes and owls blow out like candles. And the countrymen of heaven crouch all together under the hedges and, among themselves in the tear-salt darkness, surmise which world, which star, which of their late, turning homes, in the skies has gone for ever. And this time, spreads the heavenly hedgerow rumour, it is the Earth. The Earth has killed itself. It is black, petrified, wizened, poisoned, burst; insanity has blown it rotten; and no creatures at all, joyful, despairing, cruel, kind, dumb, afire, loving, dull, shortly and brutishly hunt their days down like enemies on that corrupted face. And, one by one, those heavenly hedgerow-men who once were of the Earth call to one another, through the long night, Light and His tears falling, what they remember, what they sense in the submerged wilderness and on the exposed hair's breadth of the mind, what they feel trembling on the nerves of a nerve, what they know in their Edenic hearts, of that self-called place. They remember places, fears, loves, exultation, misery, animal joy, ignorance and mysteries, all *we* know and do not know.

The poem is made of these tellings. And the poem becomes, at

last, an affirmation of the beautiful and terrible worth of the Earth.
It grows into a praise of what is and what could be on this lump
in the skies. It is a poem about happiness.[3]

Dylan Thomas, supposedly the lyric poet, the singer of the self, is
in these last poems responding perhaps as fully as any writer of our
time to the basic problem facing mankind in the atomic age, the
problem of total annihilation. Furthermore, his response is particularly suited to what C. S. Lewis would call our post-Christian
era or what Albert Camus would call the age of absurdity. For
Thomas's God, both in the prose account and in the poems, is not a
religious entity at all in the normal sense of a presiding Being
whose presence controls or at least justifies our existence. Thomas's
God does nothing to alleviate the absurdity of the position of
rational man in an irrational universe; Thomas's God does nothing
to explain death in terms of higher values. As the eternal sympathetic spectator, He simply weeps, offering none of the usual
consolations. It is the Last Day of Non-Judgment

> And all your deeds and words,
> Each truth, each lie,
> Die in unjudging love
> ("This Side of the Truth").

One can see why Thomas said he didn't "believe in God"—not the
usual God, anyway. His own God has perhaps only one function:
to make death less fearful. Or, looked at the other way round, that
miraculous force which—not for any arguable reason but nevertheless effectively—makes death less fearful, he calls God.

Some of the early poems saw death as a threat, a "running grave."
In the first London days it was understood that the poet would die
within a few years.[4] There is reason to believe that he had had
vague intimations from a doctor. But one detects no real sense of

---

[3] "Three Poems," in *Quite Early One Morning* (New Directions), pp. 178-80. See
also note to "In the white giant's thigh," *Botteghe oscure*, No. 6 (November
1950), pp. 335-337. "In Country Heaven" (unpublished) is a verse rendering of this
prose explanation.

[4] R. B. Marriott writes in *Adam International Review*, No. 238 (Dylan Thomas
Memorial Number, 1953), p. 31: "In 1935, when first I knew Dylan Thomas, he
said: 'I shall be dead within two years.'" In contrast we have Phillip Burton
quoting Thomas as saying in 1952: "I've got another twenty, or perhaps twenty-
five, years to live. . . ." (*Ibid.*, p. 36). The last poems do not reflect that view.

imminent death until the last poems, in which Thomas seems to gauge his life-span exactly. "Poem on his birthday" (his thirty-fifth) acknowledges the approaching death (four years later). Yet he meets it with an increased momentum of life:

> . . . the closer I move
> To death, one man through his sundered hulks,
>   The louder the sun blooms
> And the tusked, ramshackling sea exults;
>   And every wave of the way
> And gale I tackle, the whole world then,
>   With more triumphant faith
> Than ever was since the world was said,
>   Spins its morning of praise.

And the "Author's Prologue" (1952), with which he sealed his life's work, is written

> For you to know
> How I, a spinning man,
> Glory also this star, bird
> Roared, sea born, man torn, blood blest.
> Hark: I trumpet the place,
> From fish to jumping hill! Look:
> I build my bellowing ark
> To the best of my love
> As the flood begins.

It need not, therefore, be a mystery why the hawk is praised in "Over Sir John's hill":

> All praise of the hawk on fire in hawk-eyed dusk be sung.

His call is seductive: "Dilly dilly, come and be killed." And it is blithely answered: "Dilly dilly, come let us die." This poem about death is a celebration; "it is a poem about happiness." The Thief in "In country sleep," like the hawk, is not really an enemy. He is "sly," as the conceit demands; but he is also "sure." The dominant mood of the poem is assurance. Thomas's message to his sleeping child is that the Thief will not leave her forsaken. To paraphrase a very complicated sentence: she has a faith that each night Death comes to dispel her fear that he will leave her to grieve he will not come. Sleep is a small death, and confirms each night death's presence in the world.

My dear this night he comes and night without end my dear
                                        Since you were born:
And you shall wake, from country sleep, this dawn and each first dawn,
Your faith as deathless as the outcry of the ruled sun.

The sun, no less than mere mortals, is "ruled" (or "chained," as it
was in a draft). One's sustaining faith is two-edged: life is given
security by being bounded by death.

Death can be personified and symbolized; pathos is a ready
emotion. But a fulness of life cannot successfully be shown as a
person or a symbol. It has to be described in its particulars so that
every word upholds the assertion of value with an intrinsic buoyancy. "Buoyancy" is hardly definable; much depends upon poetic
effects whose qualities—though one can talk bluntly about alliteration and rhyme—fortunately defy analysis. Poetic effects should not
demand admiration, but should keep us admiring unawares. The
exuberant life recalled by the dead women of "In the white giant's
thigh" is so detailed and passionate that one hardly notices that the
poem is written in quatrains; the "daughters of darkness flame like
Fawkes fires still," but their longing for children (a *symbol* of af-
firmative life, if you will) is so keen that one doesn't remark how
very alliterative they are. In this example from stanza two of "Over
Sir John's hill":

> There
> Where the elegiac fisherbird stabs and paddles
> In the pebbly dab-filled
> Shallow and sedge . . . ,

one can feel that the sound of "there where" goes very well with
the idea called for by "elegiac," and that the verse ensures the
shallow is sufficiently filled with dabs. One does not count consonants to prove how many fish. Suffice it to say that the words
flick one's attention from object to action to object in a real, active
world. We might, however, be permitted one question: Is "sedge"
added to "shallow" for more reason than the sound effect? It introduces a useful but inconsequential detail—"sedge" is marshy
grass. But this doesn't prevent our repeating: Is this word allitera-
tion-determined? Does anything else help it deserve its place?

The question can be answered satisfactorily when we go further
into the meaning of "sedge"—and with the aid of the Harvard
work sheets. Funk and Wagnall's Dictionary gives a second mean-

ing: "A flock of herons or similar birds." The word has the same meaning as "siege" as listed in the *OED:* "The station of a heron on the watch for prey." It is then technically correct for Thomas to have his fisherbird in a "sedge," and it is all to the good to have this further note added to the theme of universal predatoriness. Thomas's intention is evident in the work sheets. A circled note reads: "Sedge is a lot of herons." Near it is the phrase, "a sedge of heron stilts." The poet did not use this ready-made combination. Elsewhere, however, he was having trouble finding a meaningful word to fit a much-favored sound pattern. Throughout the drafts we find the variants: "shallow and shadow," "shallow and shade," "shallow and stones," "shallow and shelves." Thomas's discovery that "sedge" is loaded with two meanings suitable for his context, as well as having the right sound, made "shallow and sedge" the natural end to the search. This phrase, unlike "the hawk on fire, the halter height," for instance, may not add too much to the serious symbolic thread of the poem; but the very vitality of such descriptive language deepens the significance of a song in praise of mortality, which can be said to succeed in so far as the diction vies with life itself in being active and many-sided.

It seems beside the point to add that Dylan Thomas died young, that he died amidst hullabaloo in New York City. His last work, *Under Milk Wood,* was a great comedy; his last words were a humorous play on "roses" and "Rose's" (lime juice);[5] and, most of all, his last poems give a sense of what it is to live well and die well, so that even an unillusioned age, "a lump in the skies," might feel that, in some inexplicable way, life is a blessing and death is a *good* night.

[5] Brinnin, *Dylan Thomas in America,* p. 274:

Dylan waked and dozed intermittently. "The horrors" were still there, he said— "abstractions, triangles and squares and circles." Once he said to Liz, "You told me you had a friend who had d.t.'s. What was it like?" "He saw white mice and roses," said Liz. "Roses plural?" asked Dylan, "or Rose's roses, with an apostrophe?" Then Liz said, "You know, Dylan, one thing about horrors— just remember, they go away, they do go away—" "Yes," said Dylan, "I believe you." As she sat beside him holding his hand in hers, she suddenly felt his grip stiffen. When she looked at Dylan his face was turning blue. A quick call to Dr. Feltenstein brought an ambulance that took Dylan to St. Vincent's Hospital.

Collected Poems and
Under Milk Wood

by William Empson

The most interesting question about the poetry of Dylan Thomas, it seems to me, is raised by Cyril Connolly on the back of the dust-cover of the collected edition. He says that Dylan Thomas "distils an exquisite, mysterious, moving quality which defies analysis as supreme lyrical poetry always has and—let us hope— always will." This assertion has a certain truth, because the arts are a great mystery, but we must remember that the logic of it applies equally to Wordsworth. The suggestion of it is something quite different, that you needn't worry if you can't make any sense of the early Dylan Thomas poetry; you had better just be pleased, because you know you are in the fashion if you say you like it, and if it makes no sense that only shows it is profound. But this theory is dispiriting to good readers and a positive encouragement to the practice of bad reading; one ought not to rest content with it. And yet a good deal of his poetry does give countenance to this lethal formula; perhaps more so than any other top-grade poetry in the language. During his lifetime he was frequently attacked for (in effect) tossing the juice around so smudgily, though this has been ignored in the very deserved acclaim immediately after his death.

In any case, he had been changing. (And, incidentally, the early verse turns on rather few fundamental ideas, so that once you know what to expect you can find them with less effort; this makes it un- like the obscurity of Shakespeare when tearing on the tripod, which it otherwise resembles.) There is a period of sag in his work, al- ready just feelable perhaps in the second book of poetry, where the

"Collected Poems and Under Milk Wood." From the New Statesman and Nation, XLVII (May 15, 1954), 635-36. Copyright 1954 by the New Statesman. Reprinted by permission of the author and the New Statesman.

succession of trilling magical lines, each practically a complete poem in itself, fails to add up. The sonnet sequence called "Altarwise by owl-light" in the collected edition is a fair example, because a lot of it is undoubtedly wonderful and yet one can't help feeling that the style has become a mannerism. Evidently he became conscious of this, and most of the poems written during the Second World War are concerned to develop a particular theme. He went on to descriptions of his childhood, as in the splendid "Fern Hill," which is not obscure at all; and meanwhile he was writing plays and stories which are fully externalised, though of course steeped in his particular tone or vision. He was just getting ready to be a dramatist, and knew he needed to, though the superb but rather static survey of *Under Milk Wood* was (as it happened) all he had time for. For that matter, as I have mentioned Wordsworth just to give the contrast of an author wishing to be simple in style, it is as well to point out that Wordsworth felt the need of the same process; he talks a good deal about the loss of his first inspiration and the struggle to become a greater poet as a result of that. We need not think of Dylan as a deluded or self-indulgent author. But, all the same, it is the first inspiration, the poems the young man hit the town with (overwhelmingly good, though one resisted them because one couldn't see why), which are the permanent challenge to a critic and in a way the decisive part of his work. I was disinclined to review the *Collected Poems* when it came out during his lifetime, because I would have had to say I liked the early obscure ones best, and I was afraid this would distress him; so I now have one of those unavailing regrets about my timidity, because he knew all that kind of thing very well and could be distressed only by a refusal to say it.

Many people recently have described their personal contacts with this entrancing talker. What I chiefly remember is hearing him describe how he was going to do a film of the life of Dickens, showing how he was determined to escape from the blacking factory and determined to send his children to Eton and finally killed himself by insisting on doing public performances of readings of the Murder of Nancy and so forth (not needed for money, only needed to make his life dramatic enough) when his doctors had told him it would kill him. You can't exactly blame the top chaps in the films for not hiring Dylan at his own valuation then; it was a question of time and one would think there was time in hand; but still the film he wanted to make about Dickens was very profound and very box-office. If Dylan had lived a normal span of life it would have been likely to mean a considerable improvement of quality in the entertainment profession; he ought not to be regarded as The Marvellous Boy who could not grow up.

Let us go back then to the early poems and their obscurity. It is quite true that they hit you before you know how, but that is no reason for not wanting to know how. When Dr. Johnson went to the Hebrides he took with him Cocker's *Arithmetic,* because (he said) you get tired of any work of literature, but a book of science is inexhaustible. When I was refugeeing across China (in 1937-39) I too had a little book of school Problem Papers, but it was worth carrying the poems of Dylan Thomas as well because they were equally inexhaustible. This was not in the least because I thought a smart critic only tastes them and knows better than ever to wonder what they mean; they would have been no use to me in such a case if I had taken up this silly attitude. All the same, there is still a lot of his poetry where I can feel it works and yet can't see why. I have no theory at all about the meaning of the line:

> The two-a-vein, the foreskin, and the cloud,

though I am sure there is a reason why it seems very good; and indeed I don't much like the poem (called "Now") it's the last line of, so I don't bother about it, but I assume on principle there is something there which I feel and can't see, but could see. On the other hand, of course, there are cases where a footnote would make no difference. Since I got back to England recently I have been asking about Mnetha in the tremendous verse:

> Before I knocked and flesh let enter,
> With liquid hands tapped on the womb,
> I who was shapeless as the water
> That shaped the Jordan near my home
> Was brother to Mnetha's daughter
> And sister to the fathering worm.

Miss Kathleen Raine has at last told me that Mnetha is a suitable character in one of Blake's Prophetic Books; but this acts only as a reassurance that the line meant the kind of thing you wanted it to, not really as an explanation of it—"That'll do very well," as Alice said when she was told the meaning of a word in the "Jabberwocky," because she knew already what it ought to fit in with. I think an annotated edition of Dylan Thomas ought to be prepared as soon as possible, and that a detail like that ought to go in briefly, but it would be hard to decide what else ought to go in.

The political poets of the early 1930s had good luck for poets in being able to recommend something practical (more socialism at home, a Popular Front against Hitler abroad) on which almost the whole country had come to agree with them by 1940. The idea that they ought to be ashamed of it, which is now creeping about, seems to be farcical. If they changed their minds they did so like other citizens; they were right at the time, as the country soon came to agree. It is untrue (and I gather that the mistake is liable to be made nowadays) to think that, when Dylan Thomas broke in, it meant a change of politics. He had much the same political opinions as Auden, and was very ready to say so; but he was not interested in writing about them. What hit the town of London was the child Dylan publishing "The force that through the green fuse" as a prize poem in the *Sunday Referee,* and from that day he was a famous poet; I think the incident does some credit to the town, making it look less clumsy than you would think. The poem is more easily analysable than most early Dylan Thomas poems, and we need not doubt that the choosers knew broadly what it meant (I would not claim to know all myself); but it was very off the current fashion. It centres on comparing the blood-stream of the child Dylan to the sea-cloud-river cycle by which water moves round this planet, and he is united with the planet, also personally guilty of murder whenever a murderer is hanged, and so forth. The mining term "vein" for a line of ore was naturally a crucial pun for the early Dylan, because of his central desire to identify events inside his own skin with the two main things outside it, the entire physical world and also the relations with that of other men. Such was the main thing he was talking about, and the point of vision was set too high for him to let the current politics into the structure of metaphors. There was no other reason for not letting it in. He really was a "mystic," as the term is used, but he would have been very cross with anybody who supposed that this meant Right-wing politics.

I am trying to consider a reader who is doubtful whether to read this poetry, so I am thinking whether I could give any useful advice. You must realise that he was a very witty man, with a very keen though not at all poisoned recognition that the world contains horror as well as delight; his chief power as a stylist is to convey a sickened loathing which somehow at once (within the phrase) enforces a welcome for the eternal necessities of the world. It is particularly important to realise this at the end of the sequence "Altarwise by owl-light," which I mentioned earlier as bad, but when it is good it is ragingly good. It ends:

> Green as beginning, let the garden diving
> Soar, with its two bark towers, to that Day
> When the worm builds with the gold straws of venom
> My nest of mercies in the rude, red tree.

I hope I do not annoy anyone by explaining that the Cross of Jesus is also the male sexual organ; Dylan would only have thought that tiresomely obvious a basis for his remark. But when you get to the worms instead of the birds able to build something valuable in this tree, and the extraordinary shock of the voice of the poet in his reverence and release (at the end of the whole poem) when he gets to his nest, you do begin to wonder whether he meant something wiser than he knew.

Dylan Thomas's Play for Voices

by Raymond Williams

Under Milk Wood, in approximately its published form, was first played in New York only a few weeks before Dylan Thomas died there. His work on it, during the last months of his life, was work against time and breakdown, yet in essence we can regard it as complete. The marks of the history of the play are, nevertheless, quite evident, and in particular the many revisions which the plan of the play underwent remain as separable layers, if not in the total effect of the work, at least in its formal construction. The play grew from a broadcast talk, "Quite Early One Morning," which described the dreams and waking of a small Welsh seaside town. Daniel Jones, in his preface to *Under Milk Wood*, describes the stages through which this developed towards the work as we now have it. There was the insertion, and subsequent abandonment, of a plot, in which the town was to be declared an insane area, and the blind Captain Cat, at a trial of sanity, was to call the inhabitants in their own defence. The defence was to be abandoned, finally, after the prosecution's description of a sane town, the inhabitants of Llaregyb at once petitioning to be cordoned off from such sanity. Thomas worked on this scheme, under the title "The Town was Mad," but later changed the action back to a simple time-sequence description of Llaregyb itself. This was published, as far as it had been written —up to the delivery of letters by the postman Willy Nilly—as *Llaregyb, a Piece for Radio Perhaps*, in 1952. Then this was again revised, the title changed to "Under Milk Wood," and performed, again incomplete, in May 1953. John Malcolm Brinnin has described the last-minute writing and revision for this performance, which was part of Thomas's American reading tour. By the follow-

ing October, having left aside certain things he had planned to include, Thomas had finished the play as we now have it.

This confused and racing history seems not to have affected the
spirit of *Under Milk Wood*, though the loss of "The Town was
Mad" is a thing to regret. It is in construction that the different intentions are evident, and in particular in the multiplication of
narrators. The original narrator, the blind Captain Cat, was an
obvious device for radio. Then, in the scheme of "The Town was
Mad," Captain Cat became a central character, so that eventually
another narrator was necessary. With his public readings in mind,
and following also the habits of this kind of radio play, Thomas
moved steadily back towards emphasis on the narrative voice. In
the final version there are two narrators, First Voice and Second
Voice, and there is also narration by Captain Cat and the Voice of
a Guidebook. Formally, this is confusing, though part of the difficulty lies in the whole concept of a play for voices.

A primary complaint against the majority drama of this century
has been the thinness, the single dimension, of its language. The
development of domestic drama, and the emergence of the theory
of naturalism, had brought themes and situations nearer to ordinary
everyday life at the sacrifice of the older intensity of dramatic
language. The words to be spoken by ordinary people in ordinary
situations must be a facsimile of their ordinary conversation, rather
than a literary expression of their whole experience. But then the
paradox is that the very method chosen to authenticate the reality
of the experience—that the play sounds like actual people talking
—turns, in its overall effect, to a deep conviction that, after all, important elements of reality have been excluded. And this is, indeed,
not difficult to understand, when we consider the nature of speech
and experience, and ask ourselves to what extent our own sense of
personal reality, the full actuality of our experience, can in fact be
adequately communicated in the terms of ordinary conversation.
Many of our deepest and richest experiences are unlikely to be
reducible to conversational terms, and it is precisely the faculty we
honour in poets that, by means of art, such experiences can find
public expression.

However, in the case of drama, it is not easy to accommodate
this kind of communication within the framework of an action
limited to observed external probability. The revolt against naturalism, which has distinguished the drama of this century, is a

many-sided attempt to get beyond the limitations imposed by a criterion of reality which is essentially external. The difficulty has been, throughout, that in certain respects drama is inescapably explicit, has inescapably to be shown. The idea of the play for voices, primarily developed in terms of sound broadcasting, is one of many attempts to make a new convention in which the necessary explicitness is preserved, yet without limitation to a single dimension of reality. It is a very difficult undertaking, and it is not surprising that the device of narration should have gained such a crucial importance. In terms of recent stage drama, narrative can be called undramatic, but in fact, on a longer view, it can be seen that in some of the most satisfactory dramatic forms ever achieved —in Athenian tragic drama in particular—narrative has had an important place. The rehabilitation of narrative, in broadcast drama, was a sound instinct, and *Under Milk Wood,* in spite of the crudity of its narrative structure, is the most successful example we have of its dramatic usefulness.

There is another reason for the emphasis on narrative. The craft of dialogue, in modern drama, has been ordinarily so much practised in terms of naturalism, that to a poet, or a writer with similar intentions, it has come to seem the hardest and most baffling part of drama: not only because it is in any case difficult, but because to lapse into the dialogue of a single dimension is so easy and so frustrating. Narrative, in comparison, is free, and in a way is turned to in relief. There is a similar turning, wherever possible, to such devices as chorus and song, because these again follow relatively directly from kinds of writing practised elsewhere. In the case of *Under Milk Wood,* the narrative structure must be seen, finally, as in part a successful convention for a particular kind of play, in part a residue of weakness following from both general and personal inexperience in this kind of dramatic attempt.

II

I have distinguished three elements—three kinds of writing—in *Under Milk Wood:* narrative, dialogue, song. If we look at examples of each, we can make certain important judgments of value. The narrative of the first and second voices is, in my opinion, relatively unsuccessful—perhaps, indeed, because it was too well-known, too easy a manner. This sinuous, decorated, atmospheric writing has become commonplace in broadcast drama, and I think it is ordinarily unsatisfactory, and particularly so in Dylan Thomas, where it opens the gate to certain observable weaknesses of his poetry. Near the beginning, for instance, we find

> the hunched, courters'-and-rabbits' wood limping invisible down to
> the sloeblack, slow, black, crowblack, fishingboat-bobbing sea.

The "sloeblack, slow, black, crowblack" device seems a nervous habit rather than actual description; a facile assonance rather than a true dramatic rhythm. This can be seen more clearly by contrast with a piece of successful narration, where significantly Thomas is involved with action and character rather than with suggestion of an atmosphere:

> The Reverend Eli Jenkins, in Bethesda House, gropes out of bed
> into his preacher's black, combs back his bard's white hair, forgets
> to wash, pads barefoot downstairs, opens the front door, stands in
> the doorway and, looking out at the day and up at the eternal hill, and
> hearing the sea break and the gab of birds, remembers his own
> verses . . .

The suggestiveness of the former piece is strictly casual, a simply verbal device, whereas in the latter piece the rhythms point and make the action, and the verbal order plays its part in character. "His bard's white hair" is not merely decorative, like "sloe-black"; it contains both relevant meanings, the man's appearance and the sense, in the word order, of the bard's part he is acting. The rhythmic stop and surprise, so casually placed, of "forgets to wash," is again serving the whole situation being presented. It is the difference between dramatic writing and unattached tremolo.

There is some significance in this distinction, when extended to Thomas's work as a whole. *Under Milk Wood* is important because it seems to break a personal deadlock, a long imprisonment in a particular kind of practised effect, in much the same way that Yeats's plays mark the development from the imprisoning "wan, pale, languishing" world of his early poetry to the fine hardness and clarity of his later work. It is a movement out of a self-regarding personal rhythm into a more mature and more varied world. Whenever Thomas touches the action of his town and its people, there is a sudden sharpening and deepening, very different in effect from the posing rhythms of the anxious, word-locked, suggestive observer.

The actual voices are very different from the atmospheric voices of the narrators:

> *2W.* And look at Ocky Milkman's wife that nobody's ever seen
> *1W.* he keeps her in the cupboard with the empties
> *3W.* and think of Dai Bread with two wives
> *2W.* one for the daytime one for the night.
> *4W.* Men are brutes on the quiet.

It is ordinarily this one sharp comic lilt, but it is markedly better than

> The lust and lilt and lather and emerald breeze and crackle of the bird-praise and body of Spring. . . .

The imprisoning rhythm is broken whenever the drama is actual, and it is interesting to notice that it is also broken for the songs, which are not set romantic pieces, but ballads in the mood of the successful dialogue:

> In Pembroke City when I was young
> I lived by the Castle Keep
> Sixpence a week was my wages
> For working for the chimbley sweep.

Those of us who were most critical of Dylan Thomas's earlier method, though recognizing that it had produced three of four remarkable poems, welcomed *Under Milk Wood* because it was the beginning of a break-out from a fixed, affected manner, which he seems to have recognized, in his last years, as increasingly unable to express all the varied life that was actually his experience, and that at last broke through in this play.

III

The main literary source of *Under Milk Wood* is the similar "play for voices" in the Circe episode (Part Two, section twelve) of Joyce's *Ulysses*. The parallels are remarkable, and some of them should be cited. I will put what in *Ulysses* is printed as stage-direction (though of course it is not this) into the narrative-voice form which Thomas adopted:

> *N.* Ellen Bloom, in pantomime dame's stringed mobcap, crinoline and bustle, widow Twankey's blouse with muttonleg sleeves buttoned behind, grey mittens and cameo brooch, her hair plaited in a crispine

net, appears over the staircase banisters, a slanted candlestick in her hand and cries out in shrill alarm

EB. O blessed Redeemer, what have they done to him! My smelling salts!

N. She hauls up a reef of skirt and ransacks the pouch of her striped blay petticoat. A phial, an Agnus Dei, a shrivelled potato and a celluloid doll fall out.

EB. Sacred Heart of Mary, where were you at all, at all?

N. Bloom, mumbling, his eyes downcast, begins to bestow his parcels in his filled pockets but desists, muttering. A voice, sharply

V. Poldy!

B. Who?

N. He ducks and wards off a blow clumsily.

B. At your service.

N. He looks up. Beside her mirage of datepalms a handsome woman in Turkish costume stands before him . . .

If we compare this with the ordinary method of *Under Milk Wood,* the technical continuity is obvious:

N. Mr. Pugh reads, as he forks the shroud meat in, from *Lives of the Great Poisoners.* He has bound a plain brown-paper cover round the book. Slyly, between slow mouthfuls, he sidespies up at Mrs. Pugh, poisons her with his eye, then goes on reading. He underlines certain passages and smiles in secret.

Mrs. P. Persons with manners do not read at table,

N. says Mrs. Pugh. She swallows a digestive tablet as big as a horse-pill, washing it down with clouded peasoup water.

Mrs. P. Some persons were brought up in pigsties.

P. Pigs don't read at table, dear.

N. Bitterly she flicks dust from the broken cruet. It settles on the pie in a thin gnat-rain.

The continuity, moreover, is in more than technique. Compare:

Mr. Pugh minces among bad vats and jeroboams, tiptoes through spinneys of murdering herbs, agony dancing in his crucibles, and mixes especially for Mrs. Pugh a venomous porridge unknown to toxicologists which will scald and viper through her until her ears fall off like figs (Thomas)

I shall have you slaughtered and skewered in my stables and enjoy a slice of you with crisp crackling from the baking tin basted and baked like sucking pig with rice and lemon or currant sauce. It will hurt you. (Joyce)

Soon it will be time to get up.
Tell me your tasks, in order.
I must put my pyjamas in the drawer marked pyjamas.
I must take my cold bath which is good for me. (Thomas)

You will make the beds, get my tub ready, empty the pisspots in the
different rooms. You'll be taught the error of your ways. (Joyce)

There is an evident similarity between *Under Milk Wood* and
Ulysses (each covering the life of an ordinary day), not only in kinds
of imagination, but also in certain marked rhythms. I do not make
the comparison to show Thomas unoriginal, though that he learned
from Joyce is obvious. The interest is rather in the kinds of speech
both are able to develop, as alternatives to one-dimensional "public" conversation. Thomas is writing for speaking, rather than writing speech (conversation) in the ordinary sense. The ordinary poetic
alternative to conversation has been rhetoric, but this is by no
means the only variant. There is the chorus of cries:

Try your luck on spinning Jenny! Ten to one bar one!
Sell the monkey, boys! Sell the monkey! I'll give ten to one! Ten to
one bar one! (Joyce)

How's it above? Is there rum and laverbread? Bosoms and robins?
Concertinas? Ebenezer's bell? Fighting and onions? (Thomas)

Or the simple, hard chanting:

I gave it to Molly
Because she was jolly
The leg of the duck
The leg of the duck. (Joyce)

Boys boys boys
Kiss Gwennie where she says
Or give her a penny.
Go on, Gwennie. (Thomas)

By weaving a pattern of voices, rather than an ordinary conversational sequence, the reach of the drama is significantly enlarged.
It can include not only things said, but things left unsaid, the interpenetration of things seen and imagined, the images of memory
and dream, the sharp rhythmic contrasts of this voice and that, this
tone and that, this convention and others. When we first read
Ulysses, it seems that we are reading actual conversation, hearing

our own full voices, spoken and unspoken, for the first time. The ordinary dialogue of a naturalist play seems, by comparison, artificial and theatrical. *Under Milk Wood* is slighter than *Ulysses,* but there is the same achievement of a living convention: the voices, in their strange patterns, are among the most real we have heard. This success raises interesting possibilities for the drama as a whole, when we remember that, in England at any rate, the ordinary modern alternative to naturalism has been, not a pattern of voices, but the single general-purpose poetic rhythm of Eliot or Fry. It is significant that the varied pattern of voices has been achieved only in the context of an abandonment of ordinary naturalistic action. The Circe scene in *Ulysses,* and *Under Milk Wood,* follow the methods of expressionist drama, which similarly aims not at representation but at a pattern of experience. Yet it is not only in modern expressionism that we find this intention; we find it also in Ibsen's *Peer Gynt,* in the *Walpurgisnacht* scene of Goethe's *Faust,* and, interestingly, in the storm-scenes in *Lear.* The pattern of voices of Lear, the Fool, and Edgar as Poor Tom seems to me basically similar, in method and intention, to this writing by Joyce and Thomas. *Lear* is an obviously greater work, and the storm-writing is only one element in it, but the resemblance matters, and the authority of *Lear* is important, if we are not to confine our conception of drama to a single-level, tidy, public representation.

IV

I have emphasized technical points, in the foregoing analysis, because we are still searching for a satisfactory contemporary dramatic form, and the partial success of *Under Milk Wood* is particularly instructive. It was not written for the stage, yet in fact, after some rearrangement, it was staged very successfully. It remains true, in the drama and the theatre, that we do not know what we can do until we have tried; our ordinary conceptions of what is theatrically possible, what is properly dramatic, remain timid and custom-bound, though constant experiment is essential. *Under Milk Wood* justifies itself, if only as this.

Yet in substance, also, it is not inconsiderable. It is true that it is very much a boy's-eye view, like most of Thomas's writing of this kind. Yet there is a warmth of acceptance in the experience, a willing return to the absorbed absolutes of boyhood, which deserve recognition in a period soured by a continual, prematurely-aged rejection. It is not a mature work, but the retained extravagance of an adolescent's imaginings. Yet it moves, at its best, into a genuine involvement, an actual sharing of experience, which is not the least of the dramatic virtues.

Is it an expressionist play, dramatising a mind, or a poetic documentary, dramatising a way ot life? In the main, of course, it is the latter, but through the medley of voices, through the diverse experiences, a single voice and a recognisable experience emerge. The play can be seen in three parts:

(a) *Night and Dreams:* "you can hear their dreams"; pp. 1-22
(b) *Waking and Morning:* "rising and raising . . . the shops squeak open"; pp. 22-61.
(c) *Afternoon, Dusk and Night:* "the sunny slow lolling afternoon . . . down in the dusking town . . . dusk is drowning for ever. It is all at once night now"; pp. 61-86 [1]

The distribution of interest is characteristic. The strong feelings are of dream, hiding, the effort of waking to the pretences of the day. Single feeling, in these modes, flows through the many voices. At near the beginning and near the end are the drowning memories of the blind Captain Cat—the private poetry; and again, by contrast, the morning and evening verses of Eli Jenkins—the public poetry of woken self-conscious sentiment. The neighbours' chorus (pp. 9-13) clacks through the day with its hard, waking judgments. The three fullest portraits—of Mog Edwards and his Myfanwy, of Mrs. Ogmore-Pritchard and her dead husbands, of Pugh obsequiously hiding his hatreds—have a clear family likeness: the rejection of love, in whatever terms—money, house-pride, cold self-sufficiency. These are the hated, woken world, set in relief by the exceptions— the loving, fighting Cherry Owens; the dreamers of love—Lily, Gossamer, Bessie, Waldo and Sinbad; Dai Bread and his two wives; Polly Garter. The town is mad because the exceptions are so many, but only because we hear their dreams. Only, at the climax of the day, another world breaks through, and "the morning is all singing" —the three songs, two of the children, one by Polly Garter, between morning and night.

It is not a formal structure, but the shape of the experience is clear. The little town is observed, but in a curve of feeling familiar

[1] *Under Milk Wood*, London: J. M. Dent and Sons, 1954.

from Thomas's poems: a short curve from darkness to darkness, with the songs and dreams of the day cut through by the hard, mask-ridden, uproariously laughed-at world. This, in the end, is the experience, in a single voice, and the chosen technique, which we have discussed formally, must now be seen as necessary to the experience. The language of dream, of song, of unexpressed feeling is the primary experience, and counter-pointed with it is the public language of chorus and rhetoric. The people, in the end, hardly talk *to* each other; each is locked in a world of dream or a convention of public behaviour. In the storm-scenes in *Lear*, Edgar and Lear are like this; the technique follows from the kind of experience. The play for voices has many uses, but for experience of this kind it is the only adequate form. In at last bringing these feelings through to his triumphantly actual dramatic world, Dylan Thomas wrote his adequate epilogue, his uproarious and singing lament.

"A Place of Love": *Under Milk Wood*

by David Holbrook

Under Milk Wood is described as a new departure by Dylan
Thomas, a literary development whereby "he intended to turn
from the strictly personal kind of poetry to a more public form of
expression, and to large-scale dramatic works in particular, where
there would be scope for all his versatility, for his gifts of humour
and characterization as well as his genius for poetry" (Daniel Jones,
in the Preface). The work has been staged, broadcast and recorded,
and is widely known. Its acclaim was accompanied by elegies on
Dylan Thomas by hands of some standing in the literary world,
and *Under Milk Wood* is taken to represent the great things
Thomas might have gone on to write. ("It is fortunate that at least
one of these projected works has been preserved for us.") According
to the standards of our literary world, such as they are, this play
for voices is an achieved piece of some distinction, even something
towards a new poetic drama. Particularly so, it is claimed, as it
represents the development of a new technique suitable for sound
broadcasting.

Under Milk Wood is the rendering of the life of a small Welsh
town by the sea from the middle of one night to the middle of the
next, by voices, and using two commentators. The happenings in
one spring day in Llaregyb are recounted, by a kind of "dramatized"
gossip. There is no main action, though there are episodes:

Captain Cat, a blind sea captain, dreams of his long-drowned
mates, and recalls his happiness with the whore Rosie Probert whom
he shared with the donkeyman.

Miss Price, dressmaker and shopkeeper, has an erotic dream of Mr. Mog Edwards, a draper who is courting her.

Jack Black the cobbler dreams of driving out sin, and makes his way abroad in the woods to seek the excitements of castigating the lewd.

Evans, undertaker, dreams of his childhood, stealing buns.

Mr. Waldo, a ne'er-do-well character, dreams of his mother, dead wife, other women he has slept with, and other sins, and in the end, is having intercourse with Polly Garter, drunk.

Mrs. Ogmore-Pritchard dreams of her two dead husbands, whom she has killed by hygiene.

The milkman dreams of emptying his milk into the river; the policeman urinates into his helmet by mistake.

Mr. Willy-Nilly, the postman, knocks on Mrs. Willy-Nilly's back in bed: "every night of her life she has been late for school."

Hour by hour as the town wakes up we go the rounds of the characters. Each character, or group of characters, is presented with a hardness of outline, and from the outside, like caricature— Llaregyb in this way is a kind of Toy Town.

The place itself bears no relationship to modern Wales, either in village or town—no such realistic relationship as Joyce's Dublin bears to Dublin. It is rather the toy-town of Thomas's childhood, and this is why he calls it "a place of love"—it is the place of his mother's love. The effect of the stylization of the piece is to make the world a pretend-place, with pretend-relationships, such as children play, with no morality or reality to impinge. Even Suzanne Roussillat sees that Thomas's Wales is not suffering modern Wales (not, of course, that it matters):

> Dylan Thomas sometimes mentions "the cranes and the coaltips" so typical of the Welsh valleys; he never refers to his period of misery, or to the industrial activities of his home-country. It shows probably his attitude of complete detachment from any economical, social or political problems . . . Wales had nothing to offer a poet in those difficult years . . . (*Dylan Thomas, The Legend and The Poet*)

Making allowances for the difference between the function of the novelist who must be as inclusive as he can, and that of the poet, who, even if he writes prose, is bound to make his effect by economy of selection, this is Dylan Thomas's *Ulysses*. We have a similar use of characters' dreams, and, apparently, a similar investigation beneath the surface of outward appearance into people's motives and compelling inward drives as we have in Joyce. Again, in the comedy of rural life, in the approach to love and death in the small local community, where contemporary civilization impinges on vestiges of archaic social forms and values, we have something comparable with the work of T. F. Powys. Both with Joyce and Powys the rendering of local life is done to advantage by the use of a local idiom, and this is what Dylan Thomas too sets out to do. But as soon as one makes a comparison with writers of such gravity as Joyce or T. F. Powys the question arises—how seriously does Dylan Thomas intend his work to be taken? Has it a serious and valuable comment on experience to make?

The most successful passages in *Under Milk Wood* are those where an amoral playful vigour is in order, where the cruelty and solemnity of the child-spirit in Thomas is not maliciously drawn out, and where he is not making a special plea for his resistance to reality. The playful vigour can, indeed, establish a kind of humanity, revealing in its very babbling extravagance an ironic perception of the idiocies of adult antics:

> *Second Voice.* Mrs. Rose Cottage's eldest, Mae, peals off her pink-and-white skin in a furnace in a tower in a cave in a waterfall in a wood and waits there raw as an onion for Mister Right to leap up the burning tall hollow splashes of leaves like a brilliantined trout.
> *Mae Rose Cottage.* [*Very closely and softly, drawing out the words*]
> Call me Dolores
> Like they do in the stories

Here is a use of Joyce's ironic vigour which combines with the critical view Thomas showed himself capable of in "Our eunuch dreams"—critical of the adolescent's wild fantasies. It is his version of Joyce's pastiche of Gerty MacDowell's reading matter in the Nausicaa chapter of *Ulysses*: the sexual undertones, even ("raw as an onion," "a brilliantined trout") are appropriate—arise from the unconscious—and they satirise the onanistic intensity of the vision, comically expanded to the grotesque.

At times the writing employs Joyce's kind of control of language to good effect, to gain a rich comedy established by verbal play:

> *Second Voice.* He intricately rhymes, to the music of crwth and pibgorn, all night long in his druid's seedy nightie in a beer-tent black with parchs.

And there is much observation, too, of how people speak, and act
—the rapid repartee of common life:

> and picks a posy of daisies in Sunday Meadow to put on the grave of
> Gomer Owen who kissed her once by the pig-sty when she wasn't
> looking and never kissed her again although she was looking all the
> time . . .

> *Captain Cat.* Mr. Waldo hurrying to the Sailors Arms. Pint of stout
>   with an egg in it   [*Footsteps stop*]
>   [*Softly*] There's a letter for him.
> *Willy Nilly.* It's another paternity summons, Mr. Waldo.
> *First Voice.* The quick footsteps hurry on along the cobbles and up
>   three steps to the Sailors Arms.
> *Mr. Waldo.* [*calling out*] Quick, Sinbad. Pint of stout. And no egg
>   in. . . .
>
> There goes Mrs. Twenty-Three, important, the sun gets up and
> goes down in her dewlap, when she shuts her eyes it's night . . .
> who's dead, who's dying, there's a lovely day, oh the cost of soap-
> flakes . . .

> *Mrs. Benyon.* [*Loudly, from above*] Lily!
> *Lily Smalls.* [*Loudly*] Yes, mum
> *Mrs. Benyon.* Where's my tea, girl?
> *Lily Smalls.* [*Softly*] Where d'you think? In the cat box? [*Loudly*] Com-
>   ing up, mum.
> *Third Woman.* and going out fishing everyday and all he ever brought
>   back was a Mrs. Samuels . . .

These are in the humane comic modes descended from Jonson
and Elizabethan drama, expressive of low life and its vitality. The
treatment of the Reverend Eli Jenkins, is, too, sympathetic and
right, a caricature, but Dickensian and sympathetic: it has even a
Dickensian movement:

> *Second Voice.* The Reverend Eli Jenkins, in Bethesda House, gropes
>   his way out of bed into his preacher's black, combs back his bard's
>   white hair, forgets to wash, pads barefoot downstairs, opens the front
>   door, stands in the doorway and, looking out at the day and up at
>   the eternal hill, and hearing the sea break and the gab of birds,
>   remembers his own verses and tells them softly to empty Coronation
>   Street that is rising and raising its blinds.

The Reverend Jenkin's poem, a good pastiche, lightly satirizes and
exactly catches the style of local newspaper verse:

> ⌐ *And boskier woods more blithe with spring*
> *And bright with birds' adorning,*
> *And sweeter bards than I to sing*
> *Their praise this beauteous morning.*

The sympathy is in the fact that Thomas does not make him
merely ridiculous. The other pastiche verses are not so good—
neither the children's game rhyme, nor the sailors' song, nor Polly
Garter's lament. But Mr. Waldo's "Come and sweep my chimbley"
is an accurate rendering of the *double entendu* verse of urban
broadside balladry. And Thomas should be praised for endeavouring to use the loose varied modes of the Circe scene in *Ulysses*, for
dramatic purposes.

Larger claims, however, have been made for this work as one of
the significant dramatic poetic works of the last two decades, and
here, surely, we must demur? Considered in the light of the deeper
moral functions of art, *Under Milk Wood* is trivial. And, indeed,
it is really dangerous, because it flatters and reinforces the resistance
to those deeper insights we need. We need to be able to allow our
tender feelings to flow—*Under Milk Wood* reinforces untenderness.
It is a cruel work, inviting our cruel laughter. We need to understand love better—*Under Milk Wood* disguises and confuses. Indeed
it makes special pleas for falsification of the realities of personal
relationships, as we shall see. All it may be said to have is comedy
and linguistic exuberance: but these are derived rather from Joyce,
often as quite direct borrowings, rather than rooted in any Rabelaisian vitality or Jonsonian irony that seeks to "correct manners"
by the laying bare of human self-deluding pretensions. *Under Milk
Wood* as light entertainment may be acceptable and even remarkable. As art it takes us nowhere, and merely flatters the prejudices of
those who live in the suspended life of what Thomas himself called
"the suspended pink marshmallow" of suburbia.

Sex, boozing, eccentricity, cruelty, dirty behaviour, are enhanced
as subjects in a comic work, as *Under Milk Wood,* by the implicit
background of suburban respectability, the interest lying in the
daring naughtiness of their revelation. The norms, or the positives
of living, expressed as the potentialities of human love, are absent:
all human reality tends to be denigrated. Sometimes the denigration
is relieved by humour, but only sometimes. And on the whole the
breathless verbal patter is devious. Why did the work become
popular? The answer is that *Under Milk Wood* would not have

had its popular success were it not essentially unreal and untender, and full of seamy hints, obscenities. The comparison with Joyce may be usefully pursued to help justify these pronouncements.

In *Ulysses* Joyce's positives are weak. Joyce's difficulty is to offer us positive values in human love without slurring into the sentimentality that one finds in his poems, *Chamber Music*. Yet behind Joyce's examination of the moral disintegration in contemporary life there is the courage of one who at least knows moral disintegration when he sees it, and fears the consequences for the European civilization to which he gratefully belongs. (The words "London–Zurich–Paris" at the end of *Ulysses* mean a good deal.) Joyce's positives are implied in the technique of the prose and his construction—the richness of the artist's verbal power, and the structural reference to classical antiquity. This is perhaps not enough, but Joyce certainly achieved and accepted the exacting responsibility of the artist, and his work has the power to deepen insight and enlarge understanding.

With Leopold Bloom, Marion, or Stephen in *Ulysses*, in the brothel or at the adulterous riot in the bed at No. 7 Eccles Street, one feels a disturbing sympathy so that one despises or condemns them at peril of despising oneself. "There but for the grace of God, go I." But we laugh cruelly at Llaregyb, the "place of love"— because "we" are different from "them." This is how the child, cruelly, because it has not yet grown to the capacity to afford compassion, looks at the world. It is this infantile detachment from mature reality which this work reinforces in us.

But first, to examine the "technique." In its plan, as I have said —"a day in the life of a Welsh seaside town"—the play has an affinity with *Ulysses*. The technique derives with little originality, and too little understanding of Joyce's purpose, from the brothel scene in *Ulysses*. The only difference is the introduction of the first and second voices to give continuity: Joyce presents the dramatic fantasia without a *compère*.

In Joyce the technique of his brothel scene, the sequence of hallucinatory montage presented as if it were a dramatic episode with stage directions, was devised for a complexity of reasons. One is that in Night Town, and at a time when the chief characters are intoxicated or stimulated by feelings of lust, or anger derived from insecurity (Stephen is locked out), the situation naturally demands a bizarre and "unreal" rendering, like that of a stage or cinema set:

it renders the sense of unreality of city night life. Again, in this section of the book the two groups of characters—those around Bloom and those around Stephen—draw together for the climax, again suggesting a dramatic rendering, as we have previously been in each chapter either "with" Bloom or "with" Stephen. Now, so that we may see their meeting at arm's length, we are given the dramatic spectacle, in which some scenes emerge from Stephen's mind, and some from Bloom's and some (which is a weakness) from the author's sheer delight in his own phantasmagoria. But the essential reason for the fragmentary and chaotic technique is that the writer renders here the climax of the fragmentary morality of the contemporary world, which permits no security of attitude to life, no governing moral complex, to Stephen or Bloom. That is their lamentable plight. Circe turns men into swine, but when they resist the simple transition and behave violently, she calls for the police: the irony of the passage is superb, and the very fragmentariness of the technique a controlling moral force. Joyce is able to explore, to present to us in the glaring arc-lights of his fantasy, some hideous and disgusting characteristics of contemporary life. Is it, as D. H. Lawrence said, "an *olla putrida* . . . old fags and cabbage stumps . . . stewed in the juice of deliberate journalistic dirty-mindedness"? At times, perhaps, the vibration is on the verge of obsession. But Lawrence is unfair even though it is true that Joyce's positives are far less assuredly present than those in Lawrence's novels. Within the whole pattern of *Ulysses,* here in the brothel scene Joyce is grossly humorous, but it is humour springing from a bitter irony and a courage of moral concern imbued with compassion for contemporary man. Lust, in the brothel scene, is rendered *as lust,* and associated with the imagery of physical revulsion. The vigour of Joyce's idiom—with its roots in English literature—preserves a positive reference to life, a hold, while destructive lust is ruthlessly explored.

To show how much lesser is his use of Joycean modes, Dylan Thomas's realization of the sea as a presence in *Under Milk Wood* may be compared first with passages from an earlier chapter of *Ulysses.* These are from Thomas:

> the sloeblack, slow, black, crowblack, fishingboat-bobbing sea . . .
> the webfoot cocklewomen and the tidy wives . . .
> the jollyrodgered sea . . .

the darkest-before-dawn minutely dew grazed stir of the black, dab-filled sea . . .

Captain Cat, the retired blind seacaptain, asleep in his bunk in the seashelled, ship-in-bottled, shipshape best cabin of Schooner House dreams of

Second Voice. never such seas as any that swamped the decks of his *S.S. Kidwelly* bellying over the bedclothes and jelly fish—slippery sucking him down salt deep into the Davy dark where the fish come biting out and nibble him down to his wishbone, and the long drowned nuzzle up to him . . .

And these from *Ulysses:*

—God, he said quietly. Isn't the sea what Algy calls it: a grey sweet mother? The snotgreen sea. The scrotumtightening sea. *Epi oinopa ponton.* Ah, Dedalus, the Greeks. I must teach you. You must read them in the original. *Thalatta! Thalatta!* She is our great sweet mother. Come and look . . .

Woodshadows floated silently by through the morning peace from the stairhead seaward where he gazed. In shore and farther out the mirror of water whitened, spurred by lightshod hurrying feet. White breast of the dim sea . . . Wavewhite wedded words shimmering on the dim tide.

A cloud began to cover the sun slowly, shadowing the bay in deeper green. It lay behind him, a bowl of bitter waters . . .

The flood is following me. I can watch it flow past from here. Get back then by the Poolbeg road to the strand there. He climbed over the sedge and eely oarweeds and sat on a stool of rock, resting his ashplant in a grike . . .

These comparisons are sufficient, I suggest, to show how derivative Dylan Thomas's poetic prose is, and also how little Thomas understood Joyce's genius. "Sloe black, slow, black, crowblack" in Joyce would have been concentrated into one word: in Thomas it is merely peppering the target without hitting the bull, and "fishing boat bobbing" is merely cliché, its movement in any case inappropriate, being too jerky. Joyce's rhythms relate closely to the feelings of experience. The associations of Thomas's "sloe" and "crow" are limited to their colours, maybe their sheen. In Joyce each chosen word reverberates always with other rich complexities: the mood of the protagonist, or the theme of the relevant chapter. Buck Mulligan's "snotgreen" and "scrotumtightening" not only convey the physical presence of the sea, but also render the desire to shock

which is a characteristic of the medical student, and which offends
Stephen deeply. The physical nausea and sexual offence of Mulligan's talk are set against that "grey sweet mother": Stephen is
tortured by the feeling that he killed his mother by refusing to
accept her faith on her deathbed, and he sees the round sea of
Dublin as the bowl of vomit by her on that occasion ("a bowl of
bitter waters"). Similarly "lightshod hurrying feet. White breast of
the dim sea . . . Wavewhite wedded words . . ." renders the complexity of Stephen's mood, the sea as a symbol of his mother, and
the life of sex which repels him.

Joyce's words, then, are not simply chosen because of a "relish
for language" or "music" separate from their meaning. His observation is perfect—compare that "eely oarweeds" in the next passage.
But the local observation is rendered with the "native thew and
sinew" of the language: like the language of Shakespeare's mature
poetry, it develops both a local situation, a local mood, the present
characters, and contributes to the wider poetic themes of the work.
Dylan Thomas's "sloeblack," "crowblack," "jollyrodgered," "dab-
filled" merely contribute to a "daft" cumulative effect of "atmosphere": "sloe," for instance, runs contrary, if one savours the word
apart from its suggestion of colour, to the salt tang of the sea, and
its infertility as against land and soil.

Again, while Dylan Thomas imitates Joyce's movement, he fails
to learn from its subtlety of movement and rhythm. "The darkest-
before-dawn minutely dewgrazed stir of the black, dab-filled sea"
has a breathless rhythm that conveys an excitement but it is an
excitement from which there is little relief in *Under Milk Wood*—
it eventually becomes tedious, until the factitiousness of the energy
becomes apparent. It goes with an emotional insecurity: we miss
the controlled voice of the true creative understanding.

Joyce's cockle pickers actually do wade, stoop, souse and wade
out *by the carefully punctuated movement:* "Cocklepickers. They
waded a little way in the water and, stooping, soused their bags, and
lifting them again, waded out." *Under Milk Wood* is deficient in
any such controlled movement: the overladen, breathless patter of
word relish becomes, after a while, destructive of our ability to take
things in clearly and exactly: "The lust and lilt and lather and
emerald breeze and crackle of the bird-praise and body of Spring
with its breasts full of rivering May-milk . . ."

We may perhaps, still considering the "versatility" and "poetic

power," examine further the much-praised opening pages of
Under Milk Wood. There are, in those opening pages, a number
of truly comic phrases:

> ✓ like a mouse with gloves
>   The Welfare Hall in widow's weeds
>   the glasses of teeth
>   the undertaker and the fancy woman

But there are also many phrases which, although sometimes
cleverly turned, are clichés of journalistic writing:

> dickybird watching (people in all old photographs in cliché talk
> are "watching the dickybird")
> fishing boat bobbing (all fishing boats bob)
> cats . . . needling
> courter's and rabbits' wood (all Fleet Street woods are full of court-
> ing couples and rabbits)
> dewfalling
> invisible starfall (the night is also "starless")
> snuggeries of babies (woman's magazine babies are always snug)
> wetnosed dogs (actually Thomas with characteristic—and point-
> less—jugglery says "dogs in the wetnosed yards")

The picture is of a conventional village in conventional language,
and the language used is subject to the same kind of external
handling of words found in the worst kind of "clever" advertise-
ment, which has no human purpose.

Besides these conventionalities there are many phrases which are
simply meaningless: "quiet as a domino," "fast, and slow, asleep,"
"the muffled middle"—these, presumably, are the "poetic" ones,
if only because we cannot understand them. But the total effect
of this "vitality" of language is in fact a deadness. It simply cannot
be taken in: the impression it leaves is of no essential atmosphere,
no flavour or quality, but an occasional felicity of caricature, a
sense of ebullience, and an impression of "clever" writing. Night,
for instance, in the first three pages, is said to be:

> starless, bible-black, having bucking ranches, be moving in the streets,
> be in the chill, squat chapel, be in the four-ale, quiet as a domino,
> be in Ocky Milkman's loft like a mouse with gloves, in Dai Bread's
> bakery flying like black flour, tonight in Donkey Street trotting silent,
> neddying among the snuggeries of babies, be dumbly royally winding
> through the Coronation cherry trees, going through the graveyard of

Bethesda with winds gloved and folded, and dew doffed, tumbling
by the Sailors Arms, be slow deep salt and silent black, bandaged
night . . .

In one line Chaucer writes:

> Night with his mantel, that is derk and rude
> Gan overspreyd . . .

and an ominousness settles over January's bridal bed. Dylan
Thomas's "vitality" is really an abrogation of control over language,
so that communication breaks down in a scattered plethora of
random expressions as merely extravagant as a child's random bab-
ble. There is, as in the poetry, no controlling purpose to explore
human reality. Of course, Thomas's audience listened, listening
for the occasional salacious double meaning: the girls are "dreaming
of the organ-playing wood," "The boys are dreaming wicked or
of the bucking ranches of the night and the jollyrodgered sea." It
is not quite obscene, but it sounds obscene, and it is for that school-
boyish naughty talk that much of *Under Milk Wood* is endured
by people who would never give half an ear to true dramatic poetry.
It is a permitted "daftness" that by being a light relief from the
dead dullness of everyday language in suburban England, leaves
undisturbed this very deadness itself.

While the "poetic" parts of the writing draw attention to themselves self-consciously, the mood even becomes portentous as it
echoes *East Coker:*

> *Time passes. Listen. Time passes.*
> *Come closer now.*

(cf. "If you do not come too close, if you do not come too close/ On
a summer midnight . . .") But meanwhile, hypnotized by the
patter and the *hwyl*, the listener or reader misses the implications
of some of the more obsessional writing that recoils from reality as
does some of the poetry:

> where the fish come biting out and nibble him down to his wishbone,
> and the long drowned nuzzle up to him. [He] souses with the
> drowned and blowzy-breasted dead . . . [Rosie Probert] speaks from
> the bedroom of her dust . . .

We only fail to notice these disturbed notes because Thomas by
his daft effervescence has reduced our response to language, de-

stroyed an essential validity. If we are responding to poetry and drama our senses should be sharpened: in fact Thomas has an obsessive preoccupation with necrophilic things, and mixes his obsession with corpses always with strong sexual overtones: here Captain Cat is obviously being nibbled in the genitals while sea-rotted corpses "nuzzle" up to him affectionately: he is breast to breast with corpses who are "blowzy-breasted"—presumably softly rotten, so that their breasts are soft like a woman's. Rosie Probert's "dust" is also her "bedroom": the intrusion on our senses is that of sexual intercourse with a corpse.

> *Knock twice, Jack,*
> *at the door of my grave*
> *and ask for Rosie*

This morbid obsession of a necrophilic kind is a sick element in Thomas's writing and marks a flight from reality in which he seeks to involve us. The reader will protest that I am taking it too seriously: yet on the very next page to the line I quote above, Thomas attempts to write his most serious lines in this play:

> Remember her.
> She is forgetting.
> The earth which filled her mouth
> Is vanishing from her
> Remember me
> I have forgotten you.
> I am going into the darkness of the darkness for ever.
> I have forgotten that I was ever born.

The relationship between Captain Cat and Rosie Probert, whom he shared with Tom-Fred the donkeyman and many other seamen is obviously important to Dylan Thomas, a point at which he is to invite our sympathy. Our sympathy is to be sharply drawn to the necrophilia itself—distasteful as it is—for Thomas is trying to involve us in his schizoid flight from reality. Captain Cat, having cried "Let me shipwreck in your thighs," is seen weeping. This is the *moment suprême* of the poetic drama.

But the lines quoted above reveal how short Thomas falls of anything approaching real drama of the *dromenon* or "thing done." The boyish view of the world, idiotically comic in places, has the interest of the boy's cruelty about adult human beings, and the excitement of naughty things seen and hinted at. But the test is the delineation of adult suffering: and here, where he attempts it, Dylan Thomas writes "Poetically" in another mode—the hortative empty mode of J. B. Priestley's pathetic attempt at poetic drama: *Johnson Over Jordan:*

> *Farewell all good things!*
> *You will not remember me,*
> *But I will remember you, . . .*

—an empty gesture far below the level of significance. What do Rosie's lines mean, beyond a gesture at feelings appropriate to dead people? If she is dead, how can she be "forgetting"? This is a dream of her, of course: but the lines take on a serious modulation (the rhythm having gone significantly flat) and we expect a general statement about Death. "The earth which filled her mouth/Is vanishing from her." What can this mean? "Getting a mouthful of mould" is a country expression, dry, ironic, stoical, for dying. But how "vanishing from her?" There is something about "vanishings from us" in a Georgian poem echoing Wordsworth's "fallings from us, vanishings"—and this kind of phrase seems distantly appropriate, as appropriate as robins are to Christmas. The origin of "I am going into the darkness of the darkness for ever" is plain enough: "They all go into the dark . . ." from Eliot's *Difficulties of a Statesman.*

But to return to Captain Cat and the nibbling fishes, there is an appropriate place in *Ulysses* at which we may usefully compare the playful immaturity of Thomas with the organized vitality of Joyce's best writing:

> Five fathoms out there. Full fathom five thy father lies. At one he said. Found drowned. High water at Dublin Bar. Driving before it a loose drift of rubble, fanshoals of fishes, silly shells. A corpse rising saltwhite from the undertow, bobbing landward, a pace a pace a porpoise. There he is. Hook it quick. Sunk though he be beneath the watery floor. We have him. Easy now.
>
> Bag of corpsegas sopping in foul brine. A quiver of minnows, fat of a spongy titbit, flash through the slits of his buttoned trouserfly. God becomes man becomes fish becomes barnacle goose becomes featherbed mountain.

Here is English prose whose effect is to satisfy us, even with a kind of elation. It may be an elation savoured with briny decay, but the writing moves, controlled, towards a philosophic contemplation of the tragic nature of life. It gains its intensity of realization—of appearances, movement, weight, texture, apprehension, rendered mental mood, from its moral intent, its moral, compassionate, consideration of man.

The rendering of the stream of Stephen Dedalus' consciousness demands a different kind of acceptance from the way we take the whimsy of Thomas's "wishbone" and "nuzzle." The concrete imagery ("fanshoals of fishes") and the movement ("We have him. Easy now") come as they flash on Stephen's inward eye in a particular mood. Not only are they realized by the movement of the prose, the corpse loosened in the flood tide, bobbing, and being grappled into a boat; but by these images the mood is realized in us. And the recollections of Shakespeare and other poets arise in complex with the imagery. Stephen's recoil from the sea, which he connects with his mother, her death, and his related sexual fears, is given us in the horrifying image of minnows fattening on a corpse's genitals, while this develops into philosophical meditation (Stephen has not given up his faith without mental torment) and his knowledge of Elizabethan melancholy through Shakespeare ("a king may pass through the guts of a beggar"). The sequence ends in a fairy tale vision of a feather bed mountain, of vast indifferent insignificance, such as the human mind strives to come to terms with. Joyce's paragraphs have a wonderful economy, and the technique by which this is achieved was possible only by a profound morality: Stephen's agony of endeavouring to come to terms with life and death in a situation of disbelief and disintegrating values, to which his literary and philosophical training give him only fragmentary aid, is subtly given us. In experiencing it, we are experiencing the moral struggle of the contemporary consciousness. The struggle is given in such a verbal trick even as that "Pace a pace a porpoise," where, between "purpose" and "porpoise" we have the floating body as a symbol of both vitality and the end of life which "moves in this petty pace from day to day," as well as the pun on "sinkapace" and "cinquepace" (the dance) from Shakespeare.

A great deal in *Under Milk Wood*, of course, derives directly from *Ulysses*: the names are an echo of Joyce's ironic use of them in the brothel scene. "Sinbad Sailors" is from "Sinbad the Sailor and Tinbad the Tailor," etc., and the rest are like a selection from Joyce's: Nogood Boyo equals Blazes Boylan, Mrs. Ogmore-Pritchard equals the Honourable Mrs. Mervyn Talboys, Rosie Probert equals either of the three whores of Bella Cohen or a character from Buck Mulligan's play, the Rev. Eli Jenkins equals the Reverend Mr. Haines Love or Father Malachi O'Flynn. Not that the characters are parallel, but the manner of naming representative types reflects Joyce's brothel scene. We have the children's rhymes and songs added, the "voices" giving elaborate "stage directions" like those in *Ulysses,* and so on.

These borrowings would not in themselves constitute a reprehensible plagiarism, for such contemporary works as *Ulysses* and *The Waste Land,* in developing new structures for the exploration of the contemporary consciousness, suggest new departures: and the brothel scene in *Ulysses* does suggest a mode of writing which can be more inclusive than the limits of conventional technique. But the use of the mode by borrowing the technique is a different matter from drawing cheques on the original work: Dylan Thomas's vitality, such as it is, is far too largely drawn from Joyce's own.

Take this passage, for instance:

First Voice. From where you are you can hear in Cockle Row in the spring, moonless night, Miss Price, dressmaker and sweetshop-keeper, dream of

Second Voice. her lover, tall as the town clock tower, Samson-syrup-gold-maned, whacking thighed and piping hot, thunderbolt-bass'd and barnacle-breasted, flailing up the cockles with his eyes like blow lamps and scooping low over lonely loving hotwaterbottled body.

Mr. Edwards. Myfanwy Price!

Miss Price. Mr. Mog Edwards!

Mr. Edwards. I am a draper mad with love. I love you more than all the flannelette and calico, candlewick, dimity, crash and merino, tussore, cretonne, crepon, muslin, poplin, ticking and twill in the whole Cloth Hall of the world. I have come to take you away to my Emporium on the hill, where the change hums on wires. Throw away your little bedsocks and your Welsh wool knitted jacket, I will warm the sheets like an electric toaster, I will lie by your side like the Sunday roast.

Miss Price. I will knit you a wallet of forget-me-not blue, for the money to be comfy. I will warm your heart by the fire so that you can slip it in under your vest when the shop is closed.

Mr. Edwards. Myfanwy, Myfanwy, before the mice gnaw at your bottom drawer will you say

Miss Price. Yes, Mog, yes, Mog, yes, yes, yes,
Mr. Edwards. And all the bells of the tills of the town shall ring for
our wedding.

[*Noise of money-tills and chapel bells.*]

One could examine several other such passages to discover what
originality they contain of their own, and what is borrowed. "Yes,
Mog, yes, Mog, yes, yes, yes," is from the end of *Ulysses:* "Yes and his
heart was going like mad and yes I said yes I will yes." "Syrup-gold-
maned" and "whacking thighed" are from the Sirens episode in
Ulysses ("Bronze by gold, Miss Douce's head . . . sauntering gold
hair . . . She bronze, dealing from her jar thick syrup liquor for
his lips . . . and syrupped with her voice . . . Neatly she poured
slowsyrupy sloe . . . Smack. She let free sudden in rebound her
nipped elastic garter smackwarm against her smackable woman's
warmhosed thigh . . ."). While Mr. Bloom eats, Dollard "bassooned
attack, booming over bombarding chords" "base barreltone." The
suggestiveness of "flailing up the cockles" (with his eyes? How?) is
reminiscent of Joyce's "with a cock with a carra" and the name
"Paul de Kock": Joyce's has more than a suggestive double meaning because the note sounded by "cock-crow" in the siren scene is
for Bloom one of betrayal. Blazes Boylan is the cock crowing over
him and the Petrine cock is to change into a cuckoo, because he is
cuckold: in Thomas the meaningless phrase seems to be there
merely for suggestiveness' sake. "Lonely" springs too from "I feel so
lonely, Bloom," a reminiscence with point from the correspondence
between "Henry Flower" and Martha the typist, at a point when
Bloom writes his "Henry Flower" letter, while Blazes Boylan is
drinking preparatory to ravishing Mrs. Bloom. The rest of the quotation is also reminiscent of the section of *Ulysses* where Mr. Bloom
gets into bed with his wife, the rhythm of "her lonely loving hotwaterbottled body" reminiscent of "the plump mellow yellow
smellow melons of her rump," etc. The "inspiration" behind the
love-dream in *Under Milk Wood* is all too patently derived from
Ulysses: to portray his comic lovers, Thomas does not draw on actual, but on literary experience, and that he does so contributes to
the quality I have described as "areal." He makes Joyce's controlled
Rabelaisian bawdy into mere urchin daftness.

Dylan Thomas's deficiency of moral interest in his characters
manifests itself in the lack of economy and order in his use of his
material. Set against a representative passage of Joyce his collec-

tions of images appear unrelated and unco-ordinated. Mr. Mog Edwards may be compared, in terms of the moral interest of a character, with James Houghton in Lawrence's *The Lost Girl*. There Lawrence's catalogues of stuffs, which Dylan Thomas's list in the passage just quoted recalls, show both that Lawrence knew the stuffs vividly at first hand, far more so than Thomas, and also that he uses them both as a comment on his draper, his attitude to Woodhouse, and the nature of Woodhouse itself:

> They wearied James Houghton with their demand for common zephyrs, for red flannel which they would scallop with black worsted, for black alpacas and bombazines and merinos. He fluffed out his silk-striped muslins, his India cotton prints. But the natives shied off as if he had offered them the poisoned robes of Herakles.

The movement and sound of that are the assurance of a writer who knows what he is doing, has "placed" his characters morally. And so the humour ("common zephyrs," "the poisoned robes of Herakles") has a keen edge in the texture of the writing.

Similarly James Joyce's bizarrest visions have a moral faculty, sustained by the control of language:

> THE HONOURABLE MRS. MERVYN TALBOYS
> (In amazon costume, hard hat, jackboots cockspurred, vermilion waistcoat, fawn musketeer gauntlets with braided drums, long train held up and hunting crop with which she strikes her welt constantly.)

Here the choice of words convinces us that the things are seen and felt ("with braided drums"): Mrs. Talboys is accurately costumed in the articles of wear for which Bloom has a perverted relish. The vision tells us much about Bloom's imagination: he is abasing himself in honor of his "crimes" but enjoying both the recollection and the abasement and guilt (*"He pants cringing,"* "I love the danger"). The neatness and vitality of language ("cockspurred," and the suggestive force of "welt") maintain a healthiness of ironic *timbre* and wit in the midst of the realization of unpleasant masochism and perverted impotence. And, ironically, again, the Mrs. Talboys of Bloom's vision goes on to speak in a high moral tone ("This plebeian Don Juan . . . urged me . . . to sin") but by certain lapses ("he sent me an obscene photograph . . . insulting to any lady. *I have it still*") betrays a morality parallel to Bloom's, and thus the passage is high comedy of a moral order—Jonsonian. The implications are similar to those of Lear's speech about the Beadle whipping the whore who "hotly lusts to use her in that kind for which thou whipst her": "None does offend, none": the theme is the general collapse of morality. Only Joyce's vitality of language preserves a positive ground to explore his horrors. Because he has no such moral capacity Dylan Thomas's vitality becomes haphazard, breathless, and overdone, its interest merely verbal.

Dylan Thomas's lack of moral control has been called (by Mr. Vernon Watkins) "a rooted opposition to material progress"; but it would seem very different from D. H. Lawrence's "rooted opposition" to the drives of our society, which never lost the tenderness of knowing poignantly, as with Gerald Crich in *Women in Love,* the individual human consequences of mechanical civilization which *all* suffer in the same degree. We miss in *Under Milk Wood* as in Thomas's poetry the essential compassion of the true artist.

Dylan Thomas's Prose

by Annis Pratt

In his early poetry and prose Dylan Thomas is primarily a lyricist, projecting his personality upon the universe, shaping its landscapes according to his subjective vision into the formal modes of poetry, fable, and myth. His early work is given over almost entirely to the recording of personal struggle, an attempt to come to terms with his faculties of reason, imagination, and desire, which provides the latent narrative line and thematic antithesis of each piece. For this reason it seems absurd to consider Thomas's writings as texts independent of biography and sources, even though the lack of acceptable fact concerning his life and readings makes it difficult to discuss his work in its proper perspective.

Until he was fifteen Thomas's experience was probably as limited as that of any boy who watches love and hate, death and sensuality, through other people's windows. The events that underlie the two earliest Poetry Notebooks, however, shattered his boyish remove and turned him, by the age of sixteen, into a bitterly disillusioned young man. Many of the entries in the first Notebook (April-December 1930) are characterized by an imitative fragility. The gentle sensualism of Swinburne presides over Thomas's first conquests, and there are even occasional pieces about shepherds and shepherdesses. From such entries as "Poem Written on the Death of a Very Dear Illusion" (May 1930), however, it is clear that he is becoming disenchanted. Disgust and horror swiftly replace the ladylove, gazelles, and litanies of boyish sexual idealism, and Arthur Machen's demons

"Dylan Thomas's Prose." This essay is a revision of portions of a Columbia University doctoral dissertation entitled "The Early Prose of Dylan Thomas" (Columbia, 1965), Copyright © 1966 by Annis Vilas Pratt. Printed by permission of the author.

and sabbath Queens replace the bucolics.[1] With the first entry in the second Notebook (December 1930-April 1932) he has begun to feel that he has given over his poetic power along with his innocence to the clutches of a savage sensuality. There are references to sodomy and homosexuality and a note of the breast-tearing sadism that is later to find its way into "The Vest" and "The True Story."

The pre-Raphaelite delicacy with which Thomas had treated intercourse in the previous Notebook is replaced in the second by disgusted anguish at conception of cancerous embryos. By the summer of 1931 he is recoiling from the vampires and Liliths who have entangled him, and in the last entry (April 1932) the devil himself has broken everything left whole, leaving the young poet's imagination cluttered with the cigarette butts and broken bottles of adolescent debauch.

With the poems of the summer of 1931 Thomas begins to achieve an intensity of line and abstraction of imagery that is quite different from the discursive, prosaic style of earlier entries. Sharp images of embittered sensuality are knit together in the antithetical clusters that are to characterize the later writing. Here, however, there is a quality of trance about the way the elements are thrown together, as if directly from an anguished mind in which rational connectives have been unsettled. Whether or not these poems reflect biographical events or fantasies of adolescence, it is evident that Dylan Thomas was victim to an unusually profound shock to his innocent assumptions about life. I am reminded of the scatological diatribes written by the young Rimbaud after suffering an "undefined moral shock" during his first trip to Paris in 1871. The affinity between the life and works of the two poets perhaps springs from their common experience of an unusually sensitive adolescence.

"It might be argued," suggests Derek Stanford, "that the real flowering of the poet's dionysian *alter-ego* took place after what Sir Max Beerbohm describes as 'the great apocalyptic moment of initiation into the fabulous metropolis.' "[2] Certainly Thomas's first short story about London, "Prologue to an Adventure" (pub. 1937), is apocalyptic in conception. His first visit to London may have been for a few weeks in August 1933, although he may have gone up to

---

[1] The supernatural "thrillers" of Arthur Machen, with their peculiar combination of Huysmans, Pater, *La Queste del Sante Graal,* and Sherlock Holmes, were an important influence on Thomas's early prose.

[2] Derek Stanford, *Dylan Thomas* (London: Neville Spearman, 1954), p. 19.

London briefly in 1931. His first longer stay was from February 23 to March 5, 1934, and by 1935 he was making frequent trips back and forth between city and country.[3] It was into a literary London temporarily steeped in the surrealist mélange of erotic joke and metaphysical insanity that he plunged during his earliest visits. He attended the 1936 surrealist exhibition, and was invited to give a reading with Eluard and others at a surrealist poetry gathering in July of the same year.[4] It was at this time that he was preparing "The Mouse and the Woman" for publication in the fall issue of *transition*, a periodical which had its conception under the auspices of the surrealist movement in France.

The key year in Thomas's total work is 1934, the year that he copied down most of the entries in the Red Prose Notebook. It was at this time, asserts Mr. J. H. Martin, that he "turned to the extreme avant-garde, to Joyce and the Paris magazine *transition*," [5] while Mr. Keidrych Rhys tells us that "he was always fascinated by its published work in back issues which he borrowed." [6] In October of 1934 his "Answers to an Enquiry," manifesting a mature grasp of Freudian psychology, appeared in *New Verse*, and it is possible that he perused Jung's essay on "Psychology and Poetry" in the June 1930 number of *transition*. In December of 1934, after *18 Poems* had been published, he began the composition of some of his most intricate lyrics. As Dr. Ralph Maud has strikingly illustrated, it was from the Notebooks of 1932-34 that he drew the original composition of *18 Poems, Twenty-five Poems, The Map of Love*, and even a few of the poems in *Deaths and Entrances*.[7] The poems in the February 1933 Notebook, which show a continued tightening

[3] "He went down for a few weeks in August 1933—this is probably his first substantial visit. In *Adventures* he talks of a January 1933 visit (this is not likely—perhaps there was a January 1932 visit?). He was working for the *South Wales Daily Post* in the summer of 1931, but he *might* have taken a trip down with Fred Janes who was to begin at the Royal Academy in the fall. The visit on which he met PHJ was from 23 February–5 March 1934 (his second substantial visit to London?)." Ralph Maud, letter to the author, April, 1963.

[4] I am indebted for this information to the Reavy correspondence at the Houghton Memorial Library, Harvard University.

[5] J. H. Martin, letter to the editor of the *London Times Literary Supplement* (March 19, 1964), p. 235.

[6] Keidrych Rhys, letter to the editor, *ibid.* (March 26, 1964), p. 255.

[7] Ralph Maud, "Dylan Thomas' Collected Poems: Chronology of Composition," *Publications of the Modern Language Association*, LXXVI, no. 3 (June 1961), 292-297. See also his *Entrances to Dylan Thomas' Poetry* (Pittsburgh: University of Pittsburgh Press, 1963), pp. 121-148.

of poetic line and imagery, represent a transition from adolescent versifying to lyric excellence. Many of the entries in the February 1933 Notebook are in a more extended verse line than those of the August 1933 Notebook, and Thomas did not draw as heavily upon them for his poetry collections. Much of the richly symbolic material of these rejected entries finds its way, however, into his prose tales.

The early fiction, like much of the poetry, is built upon the contrast of innocence and experience. From the universal and embarrassing agonies of puberty Thomas forges presentations of ritual initiation into manhood that achieve the style and the stature of myth. "The Orchards," "The Lemon," "The Mouse and the Woman," "A Prospect of the Sea," "An Adventure from a Work in Progress," and "In the the Direction of the Beginning" are tales of initiation into the mysteries of *Ewigweibliche* and into the craft of poet. At the center of each tale stands a woman, often part maid and part hag, who contains within her the struggling contraries of vitality and decay, birth and death, poetic unity and madness.

Other tales seem to be built out of an incantatory combination of Christianity and Welsh mythology or witchery: "The Tree," "The Enemies," "The Holy Six," "The Burning Baby," "The Horse's Ha," and the unfinished "Jasper, Melchior, and Balthazar" depend upon rituals which unite the world of the living with the world of the dead. "The Dress," "The Vest," and "The True Story" seem to be drawn in part from early prose-poems of madness, and though inferior in depth to the other stories they partake to some degree of their mystery. "The Map of Love" and "The Visitor," which contain elements in common with both the tales of initiation and rites of death, stand at the center of the early fiction in artistic excellence. Their landscape provides a valuable key to the symbolism of the other early tales and poetry.

As early as 1932 Thomas was at work on *Uncommon Genesis*, a short novel which concerned, as he wrote to Pamela Hansford Johnson, "a man and a woman. And the woman, of course, is not human." [8] He was working on another short novel, *Doom on the Sun*, in 1934, this one "a warped fable in which Lust, Greed, Cruelty, Spite, etc. appear all the time as old Gentlemen in the back-

---

[8] Quoted by Ralph Maud in a letter to the author, March 30, 1963. Quoted here by permission of Pamela Hansford Johnson, letter to the author, June 1963.

ground of the story." [9] The first novel was probably the original version of "The Mouse and the Woman," and the second clearly contained the elements of "The Enemies" and "The Holy Six." Although the two novels were never published as such, the chapters appeared as separate pieces along with the many early tales published after 1934. Reading aloud was as important for the prose as for the poetry, and many were tried out before a group of friends during the Wednesday lunch hour in Swansea. In the same manner "The Enemies," "The Visitor," "The Orchards," "The Mouse and the Woman," and "The Burning Baby" were read aloud to Pamela Hansford Johnson and her shocked but helpful mother.[10]

Although from 1934 on many of the tales were published in Welsh and English periodicals, Thomas was as concerned with bringing them together into one volume as he was with editing collections of his poems. By 1937 he had assembled the major early tales in *The Burning Baby* and had contracted with the Europa Press for publication. It was already advertised and the first edition subscribed when the printers balked on grounds of obscenity. A depressing back and forth of compromise and argument ensued, and as the efforts of George Reavy of the Europa Press proved unavailing Thomas began to toy with the idea of publishing through Lawrence Durrell and Henry Miller in Paris. When the situation became hopeless Reavy turned the contract over to the Pearn, Pellinger and Higham literary agency. Their good offices also proved useless, and although "In the Direction of the Beginning" found its way into a New Directions collection and several other stories were printed in *The Map of Love* and *The World I Breathe*, *The Burning Baby* never went to press.

The suppression of the early tales and the poor reception of the volumes that combined poetry and prose may have accounted in part for the abrupt change in prose style that occurred in 1938-39. This was also, of course, a time of impending war when the outer world was pressing in upon Thomas as upon everyone else. The

---

[9] *Ibid.*

[10] Pamela Hansford Johnson, letter to the author of January 3, 1963. Many of the early prose tales were copied down in the "Red Prose Notebook," now in the Dylan Thomas collection of the Lockwood Memorial Library at the University of Buffalo. It contains the original versions of "The Tree," "The True Story," "After the Fair," "The Enemies," "The Dress," "The Visitor," "The Vest," "Jasper, Melchior, and Balthazar," "The Burning Baby," and "The Orchards" ("Anagram" or "Mr. Tritas on the Roofs").

early prose tales were part of an inward universe that he constructed in his late teens and early twenties: the war not only gave this universe its final shock but afforded Thomas the opportunity of trying his hand at the more public genres of broadcasting and "straight" narrative fiction. The early prose tales are much more a unity with the poetry than the later, more simplistic *Adventures in the Skin Trade* and *Portrait of the Artist as a Young Dog* which Thomas himself tended to deprecate.

The early prose was not collected until after Thomas's death: the two posthumous volumes, *A Prospect of the Sea* and *Adventures in the Skin Trade,* did not appear until 1955.[11] At that time they were often invidiously compared to the later prose, which had become popular and even "beloved." American critics reserved judgment on the "poetic" and "difficult" pieces following the short novel,[12] but Davies Aberpennar in Wales and Kingsley Amis in England had already found them irresponsibly irrational, full of "factitious surrealist artifice" and built upon "characters and situations . . . which people in full possession of their faculties would [not] find interesting or important." [13] Many admirers of the early poetry consigned the early prose to oblivion as *juvenilia,* or dismissed it as part of a "macabre" or dark phase which was as well forgotten. To G. S. Fraser they were the "pièces noires" of Thomas's development, "one side of a medal of which the other side is Thomas's later celebration of innocence. . . . In writing these pieces, Thomas was grappling with, and apparently succeeded in absorbing and overcoming, what Jungians call the shadow." [14] Such an account overlooks Thomas's lifelong bout with a "shadow" which (fortunately for his prose and poetry) he never overcame. The life of the poet, wrote Jung in the

[11] *A Prospect of the Sea* was published by J. M. Dent and Sons in London (1955); the collection *Adventures in the Skin Trade* was published by New Directions in New York (1956). Quotations in this study are taken from the New American Library Signet reprint of *Adventures.* (1956).

[12] See reviews of *Adventures in the Skin Trade* in *Commonweal,* LXII (January 10, 1955), 262; the *New Yorker,* XXXI (June 11, 1955), 158; the *Saturday Review of Literature,* XXXVIII (July 2, 1955), 18.

[13] Davies Aberpennar, review of "The Visitor" in *Wales,* II, No. 2 (1939-40), p. 308 and Kingsley Amis, review of *A Prospect of the Sea* in *Spectator* (August 12, 1955), 227. See also the *London Times Literary Supplement,* Vol. 796, No. 2 (September 30, 1955), 569.

[14] G. S. Fraser, "Dylan Thomas," Chapter 15 in *Vision and Rhetoric* (London: Longmans, Green and Company, Ltd., 1959), pp. 224-25. See also Henry Treece, *Dylan Thomas, Dog Among the Fairies* (London: Lindsay Drummond, 1949), p. 128.

June 1930 issue of *transition*, "is of necessity, full of conflicts, since two forces fight in him: the ordinary man with his justified claim for happiness. . . . and the ruthless creative passion on the other which under certain conditions crushes all personal desires into the dust." [15] Throughout the forties Thomas was caught in the toils of just such a conflict, and he devoted neither his later poetry nor his later prose to gay reminiscence. Only a hasty reading could suggest that the stories of *Portrait of the Artist as a Young Dog,* the novel *Adventures in the Skin Trade,* or the drama *Under Milk Wood* are visions of unsullied innocence.

We know from his "Answers to an Enquiry" that Thomas was sufficiently aware of the central contributions of Freudian psychology to criticize it intelligently. It is also probable that he perused Jung's "Psychology and Poetry" in the June 1930 issue of *transition*: his feminine characters spring from within the heroes, closely resembling the "mother-sister-wife" figures described by Jung as "preexistent archetypes" accompanied by symbolism of water and submersion.[16] Although one should not be tempted to apply Jung's psychological apparatus to Thomas's work, there is no doubt that in his early prose he was trying to combine sexual and mythological patterns in a unique literary form. Eugene Jolas's experimental magazine was probably influential in Thomas's decision to construct personal myths: "We want myths and more myths!" Jolas declared in a bold-face type flier to the June 1930 edition. It seems hardly coincidental that Thomas, who had already created a number of successful quasi-mythological tales, should have presented the psychologically complex "The Mouse and the Woman" for publication in the 1936 edition.

The 1936 version of "The Orchards" shares with "The Mouse and the Woman" a self-conscious exploration of the nature of the writer and his work. The alterations made upon the 1934 draft correspond to the theories of image, dream, and myth in discussion between 1935 and 1939 among the surrealists in England. We know from his later critique of surrealism as a literary method ("Notes on the Art of Poetry" in the *Texas Quarterly,* vol. 4, No. 4, Winter 1951) that Thomas was thoroughly acquainted with its strengths and weaknesses: in these two key prose tales, which should be asso-

[15] C. G. Jung, "Psychology and Poetry," *transition* no. 19-20 (June 1930), p. 42.
[16] C. G. Jung, *Symbols of Transformation* (New York, 1960), p. 388.

ciated with such poems as "I, in my intricate image" (1935), "My world is pyramid" (1934), and "All all and all the dry worlds lever" (1934), Thomas depicts one hero overcoming and one hero overcome by the dictates and rhythms of the unconscious.

II

The last two attempts in the early prose genre, "In the Direction of the Beginning" and "An Adventure from a Work in Progress" (published in 1938 and 1939), flounder in a verbal complexity akin to the intricacies of "Altarwise by owl-light." After he failed to finish them Thomas suddenly turned to an unadorned "straight" prose style. Where the poetry written after 1940 retained the symbolic richness of the early style tempered by increased clarity of theme and delivery, the later prose shed the symbolic landscape entirely. Nineteen thirty-nine, notes Vernon Watkins, was ". . . the year in which he abandoned the struggling, symbol-charged prose of the intensely subjective early stories and began to write stories about human beings living and behaving exactly as they used to live and behave when he was a child." [17] Thomas, who was penniless, jobless, and about to become a father, was impelled by a motivation as realistic as his new style: "I've been busy," he wrote to Watkins, "over stories, pot-boiling stories for a book, semi-autobiographical, to be finished by Christmas." [18] When *Portrait of the Artist as a Young Dog* was about to be published he commented: "I've kept the flippant title for—as the publishers advised—money making reasons." [19] Thomas seems to have guessed rightly that the British public, which was beginning to have its fill of adult violence in real life, would welcome stories of a Swansea and Carmarthen childhood.

As if the tumultuous psychic drama of the early prose had become too intense to be borne, Thomas deliberately turned away from strictly inward concerns to confront the events of the social world. In "The Peaches" his autobiographical hero is frightened by being left outside a west country bar at night. As he huddles in the dark he remembers a fantasy invented in the safety of his Swansea

[17] Dylan Thomas, *Letters to Vernon Watkins* (London: J. M. Dent and Sons and Faber and Faber, 1957), p. 20.
[18] *Ibid.*, letter of August 25, 1939, p. 76.
[19] *Ibid.*, letter of January 30, 1940, p. 79.

home. This "story" contains a number of elements from the early prose: made up in "the warm, safe island of my bed, with a sleepy midnight Swansea flowing and rolling around the house," it involves a she-demon for whom he "battled up and down Wales." When the bar door swings open to emit a dazzling light the boy is mercifully rescued from the world of fantasy and brought into a world of realism. From now on Thomas-as-boy will be concerned with "me myself in the exact middle of a living story." By the second story in the series, "A Visit to Grandpa's," he has so successfully banished the dream-world of the early tales that he joins the posse of barber, tailor, and butcher in rescuing his grandfather from a childish fantasy of a death journey.

The theme of initiation into the mysteries of love, madness, and death is the same as in the early tales, but where Thomas had been involved in the struggles of his hero he now creates a boyhood mask through which he can observe others. In "The Peaches," "Patricia, Edith and Arnold," "Extraordinary Little Cough," "Just Like Little Dogs," "Who Do You Wish Was With Us," and "A Visit to Grandpa's" it is a social goal—a tea party, marriage, love affair, or proper burial—which is sought and lost. Taken as a series the tales form a litany of what a boy might call "facing the facts." As the little balloon of hope pops at each denouement the hero is initiated into a new aspect of adult life.

Thomas's ability to choose the exactly appropriate detail or adjective serves him well in his new style. His account of Ann Jones's parlour in "The Peaches" is, in its biting particularity, a model of realistic description. The strikingly new style of *Portrait* undoubtedly owes something to James Joyce's *Dubliners*.[20] In each of Joyce's tales there is a rising and falling of hope for some experience which will transform the doldrum of Irish dailiness into enchantment. The boy in "Araby," "The Sisters," and "Encounter" is being initiated into death, disillusionment, and perversion in a manner strikingly similar to that of Thomas's autobiographical hero. The failed romance of "Eveline" and "Two Gallants" resembles the breaking up of "Patricia, Edith and Arnold"; "After the Race" can be compared in the hero's quest for social communion through drunkenness to "Old Garbo"; while "A Mother," "Little Cloud,"

---

[20] "The effect of *Dubliners* and *A Portrait of the Artist* is evident in Thomas's stories, especially thoses of Swansea or 'Little Dublin.'" Tindall, *A Reader's Guide to Dylan Thomas* (New York: Farrar, Straus and Co., 1962), p. 12.

and "A Painful Case" deal with the same kind of tawdry middle-class tragedy as "Just Like Little Dogs" and "Where Tawe Flows." Both *Dubliners* and Thomas's *Portrait* form a series of stories grouped according to different phases of growing up. Thomas, however, never emerges from adolescent themes, and there is nothing comparable to "Ivy Day in the Committee Room" or "Grace" in his collection.

The difference between Thomas's later prose and Joyce's early prose is again one of dramatic perspective. In his short stories Joyce achieves the distance from his heroes that he insisted upon in his *Portrait of the Artist as a Young Man*: the reader shares the shattered expectations of the protagonist without regard for the narrator. Thomas's readers are more apt to identify with him, witnessing other people's tragedies through a combination of his experience and his hero's innocence. As a result Joyce's often acrid tone is replaced with a whimsical melancholy, as of experience seen through the eyes of innocence. As Thomas's series draws to an end, however, the innocent boy is replaced by a hero who is beginning to suffer his own disappointments. Although in "Just Like Little Dogs" the narrator flees back to his boyhood room from the tangled lives of the lovers, in "Old Garbo" he is moved from detachment to empathy through the medium of alcohol. In the last and finest of the stories Thomas's autobiographical detachment gives way to complete sympathy with the hero, who in his tragic disappointment in love is akin to Joyce's Gabriel.

Although in a 1946 broadcast he was to look back upon a seaside holiday with affectionate recollection,[21] "One Warm Saturday" affords a rare glimpse into the kind of depression with which (as the Poetry Notebooks suggest) Thomas was periodically afflicted. As he sits in the midst of the gay beach crowd the hero is moved "to an old shame and pity; outside all holiday, like a man doomed forever to the company of maggots" (*Portrait*, p. 136). He meets a young girl "at the gates of the Gardens" who beckons and calls his name "over the bushy walls." Although he longs for her companionship he is bitterly distrustful of his own worthiness: "If Venus came in on a plate," he says to himself, "I would ask for vinegar to put on her." Once more we have Thomas portraying Marlais's desire for an orchard maiden, and once more a hero feels compelled to kiss

[21] Dylan Thomas, "Holiday Memory," B.B.C. Welsh Home Service (October 25, 1946), pp. 29-38 in *Quite Early One Morning* (London, 1961).

her scarecrow sister. As if to repudiate this lapse back to the early prose world of "The Orchards," Thomas quickly asserts that the hero has "no need of the dark interior world when Tawe pressed in upon him and the eccentric ordinary people came bursting and crawling . . . out of the common, wild intelligence of the town" (*Portrait*, p. 133). "One Warm Saturday" is an appropriate conclusion to the series of initiatory glimpses into adulthood of which Thomas's *Portrait* is composed. As the story progresses he abrogates his detached point of view to proclaim his allegiance to the "small and hardly known and never-to-be-forgotten people of the dirty town [who] had lived and loved and died and, always, lost" (*Portrait*, p. 160).

The unfinished *Adventures in the Skin Trade* deals with a young man similarly determined to participate in the "real life" of "real people." Where in "The Orchards," "A Visitor," and implicitly in "The Enemies" and "The Holy Six" the heroes had moved away from the dwelling places of men into the country of the unconscious, in *Adventures* the city is the source of experience. From the time of his earliest visits Thomas both desired and feared London, and in the later prose it came to replace the arbitrary sea-goddess as a source of love and death and a place of ambition and failure. "I've just come back from three dark days in London, city of the restless dead," he wrote in 1938. "It really is an insane city, and filled with terror . . . its glamour smells of goat." [22] Later he was to recall his early visits, when he roomed with Alfred Janes and Mervyn Levy, as a golden time of fellowship and unrealized potentiality.[23] He continued to sway between desire for the city's adventures and fear of its talons until his death in what for him was the most fascinating and terrible of all cities.

In "Prologue to an Adventure" (published in 1937) Thomas attributes the infernal aura of harlots and temptations to the city. His hero, under the influence of rural protestant moralism, sees it as a place of sin where "the last tide-spinning of the full circle" of apocalypse is taking place. With its "seven deadly seas" and "seven gutters" it is, indeed, a kind of upside-down celestial city. Like the boy of the *Portrait* tales the young hero is insulated from the shocks of the environment, still watched over by the "golden sexless women" who bore him in purity at the beginning of the world. Much of the tale

[22] Dylan Thomas, *Letters to Vernon Watkins*, letter of December 20, 1938, p. 49.
[23] Dylan Thomas, "A Painter's Studio," B.B.C. TV Broadcast (April 1953), in *Texas Quarterly* (Winter 1961), IV, No. 4.

is written in the style of the early prose, although the devil's minion of the 1930-32 and 1933 Notebooks, as well as the poet-hero of the early prose, has been transformed through nostalgia into a cherub of light.

In *Adventures in the Skin Trade*, which Thomas began in 1941, good and evil have ceased to motivate his autobiographical hero who, as a preliminary to submitting himself to London as a *tabula rasa*, systematically destroys the effects of his suburban parlour. Thomas presents the snug objects of the boy's house with a realistic care which aptly conveys their tawdriness: he tears a photograph of his mother with her "pastelled silk scarf, the round metal badge of Mrs. Rosser's Society, and the grandmother's cameo brooch on the vee of the knitted jumper" into pieces until "the whole of her dead, comfortable face remained in one piece, and he tore it across the cheeks, up through the chins, and into the eyes" (p. 11). The motive behind the boy's destructiveness is his desire to present himself without "home or help" to a London which, he presumes, will introduce him to new dimensions of human experience.

Samuel's adventures, ironically, are not into sexual initiation but back into infancy: sister, mother and father are replaced by Polly, Mrs. Dacey ("He's only a baby"), and Allingham, while Allingham's roomful of furniture takes the place of the cluttered suburban parlour. The bottle in which Samuel's (thumb) is stuck is as much a pun on his being "stuck on his bottle" as a phallic symbol, while the tepid bathwater and rubber duck which are the setting of his seduction suggest amniotic rather than seminal fluids. The comic Freudian and surrealist puns are the most successful aspect of the tale, which Thomas intended as a series of "adventures" in which the hero's "skins" would be stripped off one by one like a snake's until he was left in a kind of quintessential nakedness to face the world.[24] His projected conclusion involved Samuel being arrested stark naked in Paddington station. It was possibly because the tale was turning out regressive rather than progressive, a parody on the quest for initiation which was the serious theme of the early tales and *Portrait*, that Thomas finally abandoned it. "My prosebook's going well, but I dislike it," he wrote in May 1941; "It's the only really dashed-off piece of work I remember doing . . . it's indecent

---

[24] See Vernon Watkins, "Afterword" to *Adventures in the Skin Trade* (New York: The New American Library, 1961).

and trivial, sometimes funny, sometimes mawkish, and always badly written which I do not mind so much." [25] It was probably because of this genuine dislike of the style that Thomas was unable to finish the novel.

The early prose had been built out of the inner vision of an extraordinary subjective young man. Conceived during the time of his first loves and publications, it depended upon an alternate idealization and terror of woman and upon a quest for poetic inspiration. Into it, as into the early poetry, were woven the symbols and themes of all of the readings with which he had crammed himself from an early age. The later prose, pared of symbolism and mythology, diverges from both the earlier and later poetry as well as from the early prose. As it evolved it came more and more to represent a desire for objectivity in dramatic presentation which Thomas was never to achieve. *Portrait of the Artist as a Young Dog* and *Adventures in the Skin Trade* manifest a dwindling of the lyric force which had run richly and fully through the early prose, and which, in a final union with the narrative mode, was responsible for the excellent lyric narratives of Thomas's later years.

[25] Dylan Thomas, *Letters to Vernon Watkins*, letter of May 22, 1941, p. 102.

Crashaw and Dylan Thomas:
Devotional Athletes

by Robert M. Adams

Because the metaphysical style is not only tolerant of discord but often committed to it as a first principle, critics have frequently asserted that the style invites one kind or another of bad taste. Dr. Johnson thought the radical image was nothing more than an occasion for irrelevant display of the poet's learning or ingenuity. His famous account of the metaphysical poets, in the *Life of Cowley*, points up the faults of the style as exemplified in frigid conceits by Cowley and Cleveland and in some mortuary poems by Donne which it would be hard for any sensitive reader to consider fortunate. But Johnson's blame also falls unerringly on the one image of Donne's which has been most generally taken as a touchstone of the metaphysical manner. Speaking of the famous compass image, Johnson can say only that he does not know whether ingenuity or absurdity predominates. If this is right, the whole metaphysical style may be subject to the impeachment of bad taste; if, on the other hand, we endorse the compass image, we may be left with only the haziest ideas of taste and bad taste in poetry. The image *is* incongruous; it would not have been discussed so much if it were not. How to defend it without defending other images, which are, or appear to be, indefensible?

The easier line of defense is based upon dramatic or temperamental congruity. The possessor of a gymnastic mind likes to display its properties; this may lead him to emphasize the way things look from the gymnastic point of view, until, imperceptibly, he is writing something close to a dramatic monologue. Though bothersome to Dr. Johnson, this possibility holds no terror for present generations. On the other hand, the theatrical and grotesque style may be pursued for its own sake, without the least evidence of self-display—with, indeed, a kind of voluptuous self-abnegation. A particularly challenging example here is Richard Crashaw. Scarcely a shadow of dramatic motivation attaches to his writing; he is not in the least like Donne, a displayer of himself. Yet his poetry is perpetually discordant. It makes no effort to soften or rationalize the dissonance of its images and tonalities; rather it takes great pains to search them out and emphasize them. These are, on the whole, dissonances which Herbert's poetry can soften and limit, so that Crashaw's use of them seems, in historical context, particularly gratuitous. The result has been a real splintering of critical opinion. Fragments of Crashaw's poetry appear in a confident little anthology of very bad verse known as *The Stuffed Owl*; the same passages have been subject to elaborate, approving scrutiny by "advanced" critics.

"Decorum of the subject" is also a shallow conception with which to approach Crashaw because it can take no account of the original impulses which drew him consistently to undertake "difficult" subjects. Whether or not there exist subjects which are essentially incongruous, there certainly are combinations of subjects which invite without necessarily involving major incongruity. One of Donne's frequent themes, and Crashaw's primary topic, the yearning for a physical union with the deity, seems almost to defy the possibility of a unified emotional reaction. Its inherent tensions, if pushed very far, must either explode into a joke or balloon into a grotesque. With Donne the topic seems to have remained essentially a metaphor, a bit of conscious hyperbole; when he speaks of God ravishing him or of his amorous soul courting Christ's mild dove, he is using language which as he knows (and explicitly tells us in Holy Sonnet XIII), is exaggerated and "poetic." This is merely an inversion of the sort of semi-blasphemous joke that occurs in "The Relique" where he glances at a comparison between himself and Jesus Christ; if it were anything more than a joke, it would quickly become intolerable. But in Crashaw's verse, Donne's glancing, disjointed vision is converted to a deliberate grating of the nerves, a set of conscious violent discords. The poet unites feelings and thoughts about things which have, indeed, some points of genuine similarity, but between which common sense maintains a degree of antipathy. And the special quality of his fusion is that he does not try to gloss over the latent antipathy, for to sense it is to sense the depth of the feelings that override it. The poet loves God as a baby loves its mother's breast and as a martyr loves the final spear-thrust; he loves God as a gaping wound and a voluptuous mouth, in sophisticated paradox and childish innocence—until all his imagery becomes, as Austin Warren has finely said, "a phantasmagoria . . . of shifting, restless appearances." [1] The unity of opposites, of pain with pleasure, life with death, fruition with denial, assertion with surrender, is his favorite theme. It always involves a degree of incongruity, often of incongruity unresolved, a sense of strain and sometimes of revulsion. It is precisely because he succeeds so well in unifying into one assertion, over the most intense opposition, his "highest" thought and "lowest" feelings, his most physical sensations and his most spiritual aspirations, that conventional "good" taste is sometimes revolted and sometimes amused by Crashaw. . . .

The ultimate test of one's sympathy with Crashaw's taste is found in the isolated and apparently flagrant grotesqueries of the *Divine Epigrams*; where the general economy is so sparse, blossoms of florid feeling and knots of violent contrast assume an almost jungle luxuriance. Note, for instance, the crudity of the epigram "Upon the Body of our Blessed Lord, Naked and Bloody":

> They have left thee naked, LORD, O that they had!
> This Garment too, I would they had deny'd.
> Thee with thy selfe they have too richly clad;
> Opening the purple wardrobe in thy side.
> O never could there be garment too good
> For thee to weare, But this, of thine own blood.

Blood is a royal garment as it is precious, purple, and confers a crown; it clothes many souls otherwise naked and yet represents the supreme sacrifice on the part of Christ. On all these scores the clothes-blood analogy may be made without, in itself, involving "bad taste" or the possibility of grotesque feeling. Only when the poet pushes his image one step further, by referring to the wound from which the blood proceeds as a "wardrobe," do absurdity and the possibility of revulsion enter the poem. Perhaps the oddest thing is the fact that the poem is addressed directly to Christ on the cross;

[1] *Richard Crashaw* (Baton Rouge: Louisiana State University Press, 1939), p. 192.

to suggest that his agony is very comfortable and handy for the poet, a veritable bedroom convenience, seems both disturbing and unnecessary. One might argue that there is no other way to convey the combination of sacred, spiritual preciousness with vulgar, social utility—a combination the "naturalness" of which is most clearly betrayed by our conventional expression "*Good* Friday." Yet the very choice of such a theme and such elements as occasions for exercising the witty style may seem in bad taste. Essentially, the judgment must be unitary: if the form is in bad taste, so is the style, so is the subject matter. But what, in this wholesale sense, does "bad taste" mean? Does it imply a judgment that only "harmonious" effects are worth achieving? . . .

Crashaw himself never carried the revolting aspects of his imagery farther than in the epigram on Luke 11, "Blessed be the paps which thou hast sucked":

> Suppose he had been tabled at thy Teates,
>   Thy hunger feels not what he eates:
> Hee'l have his Teat e're long, a bloody one,
>   The mother then must suck the son.

The poet here comes close to a direct statement that the Incarnation was a revolting joke on Jesus and Mary; incest, perversion, cannibalism, and the extra incongruity of "tabled at thy Teates" make the quatrain a little gem of incrusted grotesquerie. Most striking of all is the neat, swift, rather pleased tone of the antithesis; in notions not only lovely but familiar, it seems, horrid possibilities may lurk. Certainly in this poem Crashaw can hardly have intended anything but a nasty twist to the spiritual-carnal relation.

Equally outrageous to the conventional sense of decorum but comic in its startling release of inappropriate connotations is the famous stanza XIX of "The Weeper":

> And now where're he strayes
> Among the Galilean mountaines,
> Or more unwellcome wayes,
> He's follow'd by two faithfull fountaines;
> Two walking baths; two weeping motions;
> Portable, and compendious oceans.

This deservedly famous stanza reminds one of nothing so much as a landscape by Dali. The Magdalen's grief is grotesque; it distorts her out of all resemblance to humanity. The human features as they distort and break down into tears have usually been accounted ugly; her tears, as they transcend ordinary grief, transcend ordinary ugliness and absurdity. It is not, as grief, even especially acceptable to Christ. The "more unwellcome wayes" are of course those leading to his Crucifixion, but in conjunction with the cumulative absurdities at the end of the stanza they may also be taken to suggest Christ's attitude toward his forlorn follower. Her grief is helpless, uncontrollable, pathetic—yet portable and abridged because of her absurd humanity. One laughs at the images, but one squirms under them too, and this effect can, if Crashaw's art is art and not accident, be taken as meaningful without exactly being called "expressive." The whole technique of loosely, floridly extended metaphor seems to culminate in this stanza, which is ridiculous, of course, as an operatic duet between a pair of duelists is ridiculous; the art is developed beyond and in defiance of nature. But its absurdity can be seen as true to a sort of feeling, a manner, a style; and if the feeling does not assert itself irresistibly over the difficulties imposed by flesh, blood, and a sense of humor, irresistible triumph is not, perhaps, what is intended. The feeling is to be colored by a radical sense of absurdity, even to be derived, by a queer kind of negative emphasis, from the absurdity, as if the absurdity were somehow a guarantee of the point of view from which alone a grief so ghastly could seem absurd. A Christian poet, at least, can scarcely be blamed for assuming, and asking his readers to assume for the moment, a definition of reality which includes more than the humanly demonstrable; and how to suggest such a reality if not through the feelings imagined as appropriate to it?

Severe judges with nineteenth century tastes used to cite passages from "The Weeper" and similar poems as evidence of Crashaw's complete inability to criticize his own work; Ruth Wallerstein, intent on rehabilitating Crashaw, undertook to minimize them as youthful follies, soon outgrown. But Austin Warren, picking up the old-fashioned view with a difference, was the first to suggest that they are the product of a different sort of taste than conventional "good" taste, not failures to resemble Marvell's "Garden," but poems formed on a different model altogether.[2] Miss Wallerstein's compromise was charitable but scarcely seems compatible with the

---

[2] George Saintsbury, *A History of Elizabethan Literature* (London: Macmillan and Co., Ltd., 1887), p. 369; Ruth Wallerstein, *Richard Crashaw* (Madison: University of Wisconsin Press, 1935), *passim;* Warren, *Richard Crashaw*, Ch. 3.

personal chronology of Richard Crashaw; after all, the 1648 version of "The Weeper" added the stanza on "walking baths," and as Crashaw died early in 1649, one can scarcely dismiss the stanza as immature work. The purple-wardrobe epigram was first published in *Steps to the Temple* (1646), only three years before his death, and reprinted in 1652, along with the "financial" "Caritas Nimia" and an especially visceral and sanguinary song, "Upon the Bleeding Crucifix." Crashaw's taste, it appears, developed neither toward nor away from the grotesque metaphor which we consider in "bad taste"; it simply included an area of "very bad taste" within a larger area of "inoffensive taste" and rose occasionally to something we can call "impeccable taste," always provided our standards of taste are purely conventional. In less colored words, Crashaw's images sometimes contain much of the grotesque (plebeian or visceral), sometimes little, sometimes none at all. What they contain they subordinate to a purer harmony sometimes easily, sometimes with difficulty, sometimes only by violent imputation.

That metaphysical devotional poetry of this order involves two radically different sorts of taste rather than two stages in an individual's poetic development may be seen by turning to an example of modern devotional baroque. It is perhaps too early to tell if the so-called "Religious Sonnets" of Dylan Thomas will survive, or on what terms—whether because or in spite of their taste, because supported by more conventional poems, or under impulse of their own buoyancy or their own obscurity. But it is clear that enjoyment of poems which describe Christ as a "hang-nail cracked from Adam," the angel Gabriel as a cowboy, and God the Father as an "old cock from nowheres," depends on a taste which is not only metaphysical but includes a tolerance for the baroque and the grotesque.

A great deal about Thomas's sonnets is interesting, aside from their taste. Technically they are a rare treat—driving, energetic, complex, and lawless. They sometimes accept off rhyme or assonance as the equivalent of rhyme and feminine endings as the equivalent of assonance; sometimes they forget recognizable rhymes altogether. Their basic rhyme pattern is set by the first sonnet of the ten, if my ear serves me, as abcbacdedefgfg; but the c-c rhyme, originally as weak as Adam-scream, soon fades altogether, and some of the other rhymes are forgotten when convenient. The punctuation of particular sonnets is odd; a semicolon, particularly, seems to belong one line down in I, 2 and II, 6; and a question mark in IV,

6 cries out to be made a comma. The grammar as written often defies parsing, the reference of pronouns is chaotic (I's, you's, he's and
we's being used without either distinct or consistent points of reference), and the imagery, always violent and often grotesque, is based
in turn on castration, Homer, the Apocalypse, Egyptology, pasto-
rals, the Wild West, and playing cards. The point of view is explicitly that at which Crashaw only hinted—that Incarnation represents
a vicious joke played by a malicious God on Christ, Mary, and mankind.

That the topic is appropriate to a metaphysical style there is no
denying; indeed, the metaphysical mode is inherently sympathetic
to the theme, for its essence is the mingling, under stress of an over-
riding emotion, of two disparate spheres amid deliberate overtones
of aesthetic as well as ethical anguish. But the blinding closeness of
Thomas's contrasts has not many parallels in literature; for intensity seems to be the chief value of his style, and the effect is brilliantly achieved by a close, compact grinding together of images
under the impulse of a steady, rhythmic pulse and a taut, heavily
end-stopped line. Thomas evidently intends, like Crashaw, a chaotic mingling of many different sorts of anguish, a phantasmagoria
of pain and grief. To achieve this end he uses language percussively,
like a pianist playing with his forearms, creating a furious, barbaric,
dissonant clangor which has all sorts of intensity but not a great
deal of structure. Thus, though he has imposed several sorts of uni-
formity on his material, there is almost nothing about it which
could be described as unity. Images are repeated, varied, punned
upon, transformed, and trodden down by other images; but there is
no one logical or emotional development which exercises control
over all others.

In this respect, Thomas's sonnets contrast strikingly with Donne's,
or even with Crashaw's poetic style. The searching, darting movement of Donne's thought is proverbial; though the motivating and
directing force is generally temperament, the shape it assumes is
logical. Though it often pursues two or more logical directions at
once, it rarely defies logical possibilities for long, certainly never
exaggerates that defiance without qualification or ultimate resolution in a larger logical unity. So with Crashaw; though the movement of images is more emotional than logical and so the texture
of the verse is looser, the images cluster and exalt themselves in a
clear pattern of responses to the intensity of the poet's feeling. But

when, for example, Thomas in "Sonnet IV" undertakes a series of outrageous paradoxical absurdities in the manner of "Go and catch a falling star," they neither come from anywhere nor lead to anything. The one assertion which seems to derive is the poet's vision of the Resurrection after the Entombment:

> Corset the boneyards for a crooked boy?
> Button your bodice on a hump of splinters,
> My camel's eyes will needle through the shroud.

Of any other poet it would be ridiculous to say he has nothing to lead up to but the Resurrection. But here one is faced with a Resurrection which occurs ("Sonnet IV") before the Crucifixion ("Sonnet VIII") and which is not built into an event of stature anyhow. When his camel's eyes have needled through the shroud, Thomas does not see anything in particular. He goes on to discuss, with an orphic absence of verbs, the process of seeing; but he says nothing of the central actor or incident:

> Love's reflection of the mushroom features,
> Stills snapped by night in the bread-sided field,
> Once close-up smiling in the wall of pictures,
> Arc-lamped thrown back upon the cutting flood.

Whether one looks at "Sonnet IV" by itself or as one of a sequence, it trails off without either conclusion or attachment; and the accumulated absurdities of the first seven lines lead to no such resolution as their rising energy seems to be preparing for.

The fact is that the sonnets are fragmentary in much the same way as "The Weeper," but more radically; they lack not only overall form but defined relations between parts. One mark of this lack is a vagueness about the attempts at explication; most of them suffer from a hesitant, either-or tone deriving from the fact that the relations between elements—between, say, the bagpipe-breasted sirens and the Crucifixion, or the white bear quoting Virgil and two-gunned Gabriel—has been defined by the critic, not the poet. "Maybe Thomas means this or perhaps that." The implication is that it does not matter much which alternative one chooses; and since in a sense, Thomas himself has made no definite choice, it isn't really up to the reader to choose either. All this is well and good, a poet may certainly enrich his poem by meaning two things at once, but he will certainly confuse it by meaning sixteen things at once, without making clear the relation between them. The most capacious and unstrained form of unity that can be seen is undoubtedly the best—and this it is undoubtedly the reader's, or the critic's, responsibility to discover. It is even conceivable that the full meaning of a poem may be understood only by looking at it in several distinct, even incompatible ways, successively. No price is too high to pay for genuine richness. But a multitude of hazily related, or unrelated, particulars may produce not the impression of richness but that of monotony. And then if the whole structural unity of the poem is resolved into a single, drumming, extravagant antithesis, along with all hope for variety of effect, the greater part of one's notion of structural decorum must go by the board. There are very few poems in the canon which give such an effect of blind, swirling energy unrelated to a total structure as these "Religious Sonnets" of Dylan Thomas. They remind one of the paintings of Jackson Pollock—a vortex of energy, totally unmechanical, immediate and violent, with all the raw ends of the creator's nerves showing, yet not really distinguishable one from the other.

Is it a defensible aesthetic position to say that so long as each individual section of his poem is built on sufficiently violent and intensive contrasts the poet need provide no structure of mood, tone, imagery, temporal order, or grammatical assertion? The distinctions here are quanitative, not absolute; but there certainly comes a point where confused poems seem to represent the best approach to confusion and dull novels the most exquisite expression of dullness. This is the imitative fallacy with a vengeance; in matters of dullness and confusion we condemn it easily enough, but when questions of grotesque and incongruous taste are at issue our standards somehow become less rigid. Perhaps we have really learned that there are more universes to be inhabited than are dreamt of in any one philosophy. But the world of those who divide taste into "good" and "bad" has strictly unitary implications. To be applied at all, the concepts will have to be applied wholesale, and within a rather rigid conventional framework. If the central theme of a poem is not subject to the imputation of bad taste, no meaning can attach to a condemnation of ornaments which may be perfectly appropriate to, and expressive of, that theme. When the theme becomes incongruity itself, we are close to a no-man's-land where all standards of taste are conditional on one's "taste" for the actual thing being experienced. The real complaint against metaphysical poetry of the intense and unresolved variety is not that it assumes one sort of taste as a touchstone in opposition to all others but that it casts a doubt on the general relevance of *any* single standard of taste. It makes explicit that dependence of the poem on the reader's imaginative experience which is only implicit in conventional poetry, and it does so by presuming a special condition in the reader that is too widespread to be called private but a good deal less than universal. . . .

Thus critics cannot place one decorum above another without exalting one subject-matter above another, so that all systems of critical value rest ultimately on systems of general value which are only remotely comparable, if at all. This is a discouraging observation for critics. But writers are not apt to be so seriously disturbed by an all-but-universal relativism. Unprincipled creatures at best, they can rest content with a merest fragment of that value-hierarchy at which the critics' Babel is constantly building. Thomas quite properly welcomed the chance to judge for himself how close poetry can come to the psychopathic and still survive. He drew the line closer than poets since Blake have generally drawn it; there are plenty of reasons for thinking *Angst* so permanent and general a condition of thinking mankind as to more than justify his choice.

Dylan Thomas

by John Bayley

The poetry of Dylan Thomas has obviously much in common with that of Rimbaud and Hopkins, and with the word expedients of conventional surrealism as well. Any attempt to interpret and appreciate it, therefore, should perhaps start from the standpoint of language: we are most likely to find what Thomas is getting at, what he wants to say, if we first examine the linguistic forms in which he has been driven to say it.

Words, single words, are far more important in Thomas's poetry than in that of Yeats or Auden. We should expect this. Although Auden has said that a "passionate love of words" is a pre-requisite for every poet, his own highly referential language depends much more on that "natural momentum of syntax" which Yeats sought for so diligently, than on the individual word. The norm of both Yeats's and Auden's poetry is fluency, conversation: the norm of Thomas's is incantation, the single word as thing, dropped on to the page. Keeping in mind this basic distinction, we might seek a first foothold on the difficulties of Thomas's poetry by a comparison of some of his adjectives with those referential ones whose operation we have already discussed.

(1) Socket and grave, the brassy blood,
    Flower, flower, all all and all.
(2) Forged in man's minerals, the brassy orator
    Laying my ghost in metal. . . .
(3) My Egypt's armour buckling in its sheet,
    I scrape through resin to a starry bone
    And a blood parhelion.

(4) Turning a petrol face blind to the enemy
Turning the riderless dead by the channel wall.

(5) Where once the waters of your face
Spun to my screws

(6)   . . . the nitric stain
On fork and face.

(7) The night is near,
A nitric shape that leaps her, time and acid;

(8) On field and sand
The twelve triangles of the cherub wind
Engraving going.

(9) My veins flowed with the Eastern weather;
Ungotten I knew night and day.

(10) Consider now the old effigy of time, his long beard
whitened by an Egyptian sun, his bare feet watered
by the Sargasso sea.

(11) . . . So fast I move defying time, the quiet gentleman
Whose beard wags in Egyptian wind.

(12) In the poles of the year
When black birds died like priests in the cloaked hedge row
And over the cloth of counties the far hills rode near.

(13) Once it was the colour of saying
Soaked my table the uglier side of a hill
With a capsized field where a school sat still
And a black and white patch of girls grew playing.

(14) The chitterlings of a clock . . .

(15) Though the town below lay leaved with October blood.

(16) My busy heart who shudders as she talks
Sheds the syllabic blood and drains her words.

(17) The puffed birds hopping and hunting, the milkmaids
Gentle in their clogs over the fallen sky.

If we analyse the individual words in these extracts we are puzzled
by the wide variation of effect which they reveal. Some show the
poetic pregnancy, simultaneously existing as satisfying "thing" and
as subtle indicator, which we expect in more straightforward
poetry. In extracts 8 and 12 all the words—"cloth," "cloaked,"
"cherub"—have this quality, and engraving combines smoothly
and comprehensively the suggestions of the wind furrowing snow
or sand, and the lines etched in relief on a sundial's face (it is an
obvious truth of romantic poetry that exact words usually "suggest" far more powerfully than vague ones). "Chitterlings" is as

surprising as Valéry's "scrupulous," and as effective. "Puffed" in 17 is similarly exact, and "syllabic" in 16 suggests both the prophetic touch of "sibyl" or "sibylline" and is also a language metaphor comparable to "the reasons of the heart." "Leaved with October blood" is a simple conceit or metaphor for autumn leaves, as is "the fallen sky" for snow-covered ground. "Capsized" in 13 is a more metaphysical usage that would have delighted Shakespeare or Donne; the pun has a lyrical wit, and the precision of the verbs "sat" and "grew" indicates the blend of repose and restless movement which haunts Thomas's vision of adolescence. 5 is similarly a metaphorical conceit. 4, 10, and 11 are examples of a private but coherent and consistent image, like Blake's star and tiger; "Egyptian" and "eastern" are always images of time for Thomas. "Nitric" and "brassy" are more puzzling: "nitric" again seems to have associations for Thomas of time and wearing away, but its use in the second instance is confusing, though the word "acid" gives a kind of dislodged clue. "Brassy" as applied to orator is clear enough, but what is its relation to blood, and why "starry" bone? Language here seems to have left the referential for the absolute pole; sign has become thing, and such faint referential echoes as we can catch are necessarily uncertain, and do not lead us with any inevitability. A "parhelion" we find, on consulting the dictionary, is "a spot on a solar halo at which the light is intensified . . . a mock sun." We look in vain here for any metaphysical clue; Thomas does not appear to use the word as a meaningful illustration, like Donne's intelligences and spheres, but for its sound, and its exotic unfamiliarity. A stock Romantic usage in fact, such as one might find in Swinburne, or, in a rather different way, in Yeats. "Riderless" is tolerably easy: again the associations are romantic—Riders to the Sea, the riding ship,—the phrase is as eloquent for the dead here as it is for the unborn in the line,

> A limp and riderless shape to leap nine thinning months

And it reminds us of one of the most beautiful of all Thomas's compressed epithets, "the riding Thames," in the poem "A Refusal to Mourn," which gives the feeling of the river's immortality as a part of the child's death.

But the phrase "a petrol face" is implacably opaque. In this context the word does not seem alive at all, though the questing associative faculty might revolve the images of the sea bird "petrel," or of the stain of oil on top of the water. I suspect, though, that the very inertia of the word may be the reason for its presence here: after a succession of "live" words (e.g. "the *haring* snail" in the preceding stanza), the intrusion of a "dead" one may be the effect intended—the closest parallel that language can offer for an actual physical apprehension of death.

Though they are not the most complex that could be found in his work, these examples, particularly the last, do give us, I think, a sense of the issues involved, and of how devious and varied is the task which Thomas sets to the resources of language. They help to explain, too, the bewilderment and frustration which even the most careful and devoted reader cannot help feeling on occasion. Scarcely has he accustomed himself to one kind of linguistic usage—say the conventional exactness of "capsized field," or "blood-counting clock"—when he has to adjust himself to an entirely different one. It is as if the attitudes to language of Donne, Blake, and Swinburne were all to be encountered in the same poem. The revival of interest in metaphysical technique has left its mark on Thomas, and he is not the only modern poet in whom the task of "prehending language emotionally and intellectually at once" (the comment is Auden's) imposes a severe strain upon the reader. In her book on the imagery of the Metaphysicals,[1] Miss Tuve has suggested that one secret of the strength and clarity of their poetry is that their images omit "all but the one prick of the point of connection" which the sense requires. In other words, where a true metaphysical use of language is concerned, in such a phrase as

> Age is love's timber, youth his underwood,

we are not to dwell upon either the "thingy" or the associative nature of the words "timber" and "underwood," but simply to grasp the meaning towards which they point as metaphors. In a romantic use of language, the significance of the words as metaphors would be weak or vague, and their suggestive power correspondingly dwelt upon. The reaction of the modern poet—and it is a very understandable one—is, why not have both? Indeed, William Empson, in a review of Miss Tuve's book, questioned whether this insulation of imagery could exist, and implied that to write or read poetry as if it could was to impoverish the scope of

[1] Rosamond Tuve, *Elizabethan and Metaphysical Imagery,* Chicago: University of Chicago Press, 1947.

poetic effect. "If you can't explain what seems to you a good line and still decide to print it, you are trusting that the reader has the same feelings as yourself." The use of the word "feelings" here is obviously suspect: Empson makes use of a romantic terminology which is out of place in speaking of Metaphysical poetry in the historical sense. Donne would not have appealed to his readers' feelings to decide on the decorum of an image which seems to us to do inexplicably more than indicate a metaphorical connection— he would have appealed to their wit and reason. The answer is perhaps that the insulation process may take place if the reader is linguistically habituated to it: and making associations in poetry is equally a habit rather than a necessity, as is sharing the "feelings" of a poet who has let a line stand although he cannot explain it. All readers who are brought up on romantic poetry find difficulty in appreciating the native qualities of the Metaphysicals, and are tempted to extract from them whatever seems to fall in with their own habits of reading: historically speaking we can be fairly sure that the reading habits of the poet's audience in the seventeenth and the nineteenth centuries were in fact very different. But now we are being asked to combine the two. If our tastes are eclectic, and we are seasoned in all sorts of poetry, this should be ideal, but it can only happen effectively if all the poem, and the images in it, can be read both "metaphysically" and "romantically." Problems will occur if some of the poem seems to show metaphysical "sense" and other parts associational "sound," or some other type of linguistic effect. And this, as our examples show, does occur in Thomas's poetry.

The result is a degree of warring, and sometimes damaging, comparison. It is only with great agility and understanding that the reader can accept such varying usages as each functional and necessary in its kind: the tendency at first is to react sharply to the "transparent" and referential clues, and gloss helplessly over the more opaque and difficult words and passages. In consequence the wholeness of the poem remains difficult to grasp; it is as if—to adopt a rough-and-ready metaphor—our progress through it was not a smooth expanding flow, but rather an obstacle race at different levels—scrambling over objects, falling into holes, and clambering painfully out again to nerve ourselves for a jump across a chasm or a tightrope walk between two trees. In the course of this uneven journey the reader has the right to ask himself whether

Thomas's use of language is not simply good at some points and bad at others; whether, in fact, the whole procedure is not a hit-or-miss method based on an elementary use of poetic "pregnancy"; and in which Thomas is a careless genius often blessed with good luck, instead of a laborious craftsman obsessed with the ways in which language can be brought more and more directly into contact with feelings and things.

I believe that the second view is the right one, but it is a difficult thing to demonstrate. The critical uncertainty which must still be felt about Thomas's real status as a poet arises from the fact that we still do not know whether language is capable of what he tried to do with it; or rather whether the consciousness of the receiver can adapt itself to such a variety of linguistic uses and such a multiplicity of verbal stimuli. Probably it can. In its necessary evasion of a status quo, language in its aesthetic uses is always tending to become more complex, to demand a greater degree of vigilance and delicacy in its apprehension. Acting, as it does, as a kind of mirror of the trained self-consciousness, it is always seeking to enlarge that consciousness, to force upwards into the light of its expression the inchoate mass of vague awareness which lies below the level of thought and speech. Thanks to theoreticians like Freud and Jung, the degree of self-consciousness which we have already attained about our submerged selves is remarkable, perhaps frightening— one wonders where such exploration is going to end, if not in a blank limbo of unfruitful understanding. The language of poetry can perhaps act, in a strange way, as a kind of vitaliser of such understanding, as a means to keep it alive and kicking. Although, by its very nature, poetic language is bound to turn feeling into thought (as an early surrealist remarked, *"La pensée se forme dans la bouche"*—words must become thoughts in order to be words), when the process takes place in poetry we retain the mysteriousness and the joyfully hidden quality which existed before the transformation; the sense of thoughts that do lie too deep for words, even though—by some miracle—we are reading those words on the printed page. Poetry can thus act not only as an enlightener—and Thomas often spoke of his obsession with making dark things clear and plain—but as a corrective to enlightenment, as a means of combating the sterile progress of self-consciousneess. In his autobiography Arthur Koestler tells a story of a woman with a mental disorder who had hallucinations: she had been much analysed and knew exactly what the significance of her visions was in terms of childhood hates, sex fears, etc., and she accepted with a dreary finality the accuracy of the interpretation; but it gave her no help, and as her visions persisted the lucidity with which she could now objectify them brought her nothing but despair, in spite of the affirmatory and liberal tone her Jungian analyst attempted to impart to the enlightening process. The bringing of the hidden to light by poetry is a very different order of experience, requiring not a ready-made general vocabulary, but its own fibre of thought and language which appears—even though this may be an illusion —to have been dragged up from the same depths as the experience itself.

This exploration and bringing to light of the dark interior, the "unknown modes of being," was once the primal Romantic aim, the chief preoccupation of Wordsworth and Coleridge. Although any comparison of these two with Thomas would obviously, at this stage, be ridiculously premature, it is probably true that no other poet since them has shared their interests so much as he. Although we cannot tell as yet what size of poet he is (and he may yet be judged as intrinsically slight as Laforgue or Clare or Owen), yet he has the absorption and the single-mindedness of the great Romantics. He shows the same steady inward gaze as Wordsworth, the same inspired egotism, but whereas Wordsworth attempted to trace the growth and movements of his mind in the plain lucid diction which he thought proper to poetry and which he had in fact inherited from the eighteenth century, Thomas tries to get at the mystery of his own growth and being by means of his own highly personal idioms and image clusters. Not that Wordsworth's language—so far as its effect on the reader is concerned—is like the normal language of rational intercourse or prose. As F. R. Leavis has pointed out, although Wordsworth's meditation appears to be "preoccupied with a scrupulous nicety of statement," its overall effect is in fact largely independent of this semblance of analysis. It wakens—to borrow Shelley's phrase—"a sort of thought in sense": its conventionality of detail leads the reader on to perceptions of a deeper, non-rational kind. And this process has one enormous advantage which Thomas's poetry conspicuously lacks. When it is necessary for Wordsworth to make some direct statement, to link the stages of his poem by some purely intellectual armature, he can do it without any incongruity and without any obvious switch to a different order of understanding. He can, to put it baldly, draw a moral in the same language in which he has conveyed a vision. Moreover he can attempt to relate his own personal experiences to the general social background, because there is nothing in his language which is inapplicable to such a background: it is one of the great strengths of Wordsworth's and Coleridge's Romanticism that they admit no division between the hidden depths they explore, and the human situation in its widest and most social sense.

It is worth illustrating this point by means of a famous passage from *The Prelude*. In the passage in Book Twelve beginning "There are in our existence spots of time . . ." Wordsworth tells how one of his chief "visitings of imaginative power" befell him when he was lost on a stretch of lonely moor where a gallows had once stood. Running away in panic he sees a girl with a pitcher on her head.

> It was, in truth
> An ordinary sight; but I should need
> Colours and words that are unknown to man,
> To paint the visionary dreariness
> Which, while I looked all round for my lost guide,
> Invested moorland waste and naked pool,
> The beacon crowning the lone eminence,
> The female and her garments vexed and tossed
> By the strong wind. When, in the blessed hours
> Of early love, the loved one at my side,
> I roamed in daily presence of this scene,
> Upon the naked pool and dreary crags,
> And on the melancholy beacon fell
> A spirit of pleasure and youth's golden gleam;
> And think ye not with radiance more sublime
> For these remembrances, and for the power
> They had left behind? So feeling comes in aid
> Of feeling, and diversity of strength
> Attends us, if but once we have been strong.
> Oh! mystery of man, from what a depth
> Proceed thy honours. I am lost, but see
> In simple childhood something of the base
> On which thy greatness stands; but this I feel,
> That from thyself it comes, that thou must give
> Else never canst receive. The days gone by
> Return upon me almost from the dawn

> Of life: the hiding-places of man's power
> Open; I would approach them, but they close.
> I see by glimpses now; when age comes on,
> May scarcely see at all; and I would give,
> While yet we may, as far as words can give,
> Substance and life to what I feel.

The transitions here between the naked event described, and the commentary on it, are masterly. The retrospection (and Wordsworth's finest poetry is almost always avowedly retrospective) does not in the least detract from the shock and thrill of the experience, and the impact that it makes on the reader. There is a breadth and humility in his attitude which reaches its climax in the calm simplicity of that "I am lost," all the more effective for being in no way gestured about or dwelt on—indeed a hasty reading might overlook it. In two places Wordsworth explicitly disclaims the efficacy of language to render what he felt: the poetry is not only retrospective but an admitted paraphrase. None the less it comes to us directly. Even the impersonal, unstressed diction (the bleak "female" which was substituted for "woman" in the 1805 edition) has its share in the impression: and the phase which trembles on the verge of cliché. "A spirit of pleasure and youth's golden dream," contrasts with the "visionary dreariness" to render the mysterious interrelation between terror and happiness—even a light, conventional happiness—which the poet discerns.

Now, the experiences that Thomas tries to bring to light are not very different from these, but he has none of Wordsworth's social and retrospective breadth. Perhaps he does not want it. He is writing in a poetic climate about which Auden, as we have already noted, remarked in 1927—"Emotion is no longer necessarily to be analysed by 'recollection in tranquillity': it is to be prehended emotionally and intellectually at once." It is this arduous synthesis that Thomas is unconsciously trying to achieve, and the absence of retrospection in his poetry—its unswerving truth to what is going on rather than to what *has* gone on—throws considerable light on its linguistic difficulty. The counterpart to our embarrassment over the different ways in which he uses words, the different "meanings" he imposes on them, is the way in which darkness and light, experience and explanation, are often present together in the same poem, but in an unfused state: when synthesis fails the poem is troubled (in a way Wordsworth's can never be) by the obscurity of its direct "stuff" and the comparative banality of an emergent gloss or commentary on it. Sometimes, in fact, we suffer a positively uneasy feeling when Thomas *is* clear. "Is this what all the business is about?" is our reaction. When the poem, instead of being taken in at some deep, almost wordless, level of the mind, brings itself to the rational surface, it loses its lustre like a stone from a rock pool exposed to the air. Working the whole movement of a poem at different levels is as difficult and dangerous a feat as using words in different ways and with different kinds of emphasis. Discrepancies in the poem's wholeness are almost inevitable.

This explains, too, the contrast between the rich unlimited feel of some of his poems, and the startlingly finite nature of others—a contrast which has led to the conclusion of some critics that Thomas had very little "to say," and that when he had, in a muffled but compelling manner, got it out, there remained nothing for him to fall back on but the virtuosity with words which he had acquired in the process. Poems like "The hand that signed the paper," "This Side of the Truth," "We lying by seasand," "The Hunchback in the Park," have this finished quality, as of a perception well handled and expertly rounded off, which would be quite in keeping with the bent of Auden or even—to take a very different example—W. H. Davies, but which do have an effect of incongruity in the context of Thomas's work. Versatility is oddly disturbing in a poet whose strength and linguistic originality seem to lie in a kind of inspired *groping*—"groping for matter under the dog's plate." And this groping delicacy—it is one of the things that nake it so good when it works—teeters continually on a knife-edge between complete opacity and the inertia of ordinary "sense." To appear to be striving after sense, as Thomas sometimes does, to be saying something with difficulty which is simple enough to be said in an approximate form with ease—that is a nemesis which his linguistic approach cannot always avoid. Consider the first two stanzas of "Out of the sighs."

> Out of the sighs a little comes,
> But not of grief, for I have knocked down that
> Before the agony; the spirit grows,
> Forgets, and cries;
> A little comes, is tasted and found good;
> All could not disappoint
> There must, be praised, some certainty,

>   If not of loving well, then not,
>   And that is true after perpetual defeat.
>
>   After such fighting as the weakest know,
>   There's more than dying;
>   Lose the great pains or stuff the wound,
>   He'll ache too long
>   Through no regret of leaving woman waiting
>   For her soldier stained with spilt words
>   That spill such acrid blood.

The hesitant, rather awkward statement of the first stanza, with its marked absence of images, makes its point circuitously, almost timidly: "A little," something positive, something worth having, emerges from the sadness and the impoverishment of growing up, of living; even unhappy love supports this positive residue. In the next stanza the point is developed. Our reaction to the wounds of life is to retain this as it were reservoir of feeling, of neutral contentment or grief, which is indifferent to the original conflicts and causes—the "woman waiting"—and which is in some way associated with the poet's capacity to name what has happened to him, to put it into words. The association of words with blood and feeling—the mention of them in the same breath and as if they were the same order of things—is characteristic of Thomas and we must return to it: it is worth comparing it here with the conventional statement of Wordsworth that words, a different method of perception, can only be put alongside what he once felt, as an approximate description.

   The poem continues:

>   Were that enough, enough to ease the pain,
>   Feeling regret when this is wasted
>   That made me happy in the sun,
>   How much was happy while it lasted,
>   Were vaguenesses enough and the sweet lies plenty,
>   The hollow words could bear all suffering . . .
>
>   Were that enough, bone, blood, and sinew,
>   The twisted brain, the fair-formed loin,
>   Groping for matter under the dog's plate,
>   Man should be cured of distemper.
>   For all there is to give I offer:
>   Crumbs, barn, and halter.

"The little" now emerges more clearly as that neutral over-plus of vitality which makes one "happy in the sun"; if this state of equilibrium, which the poet now connects with "vaguenesses" and "sweet lies," were enough for living, then words—which inhabit this province—would be more powerful than they are. "Hollow" suggests not only impotence but the rounded, protected state, succeeding effort and grief, in which words operate. Words here *are* being looked at as something retrospective, and this seems to conflict with their position in the preceding stanza: as the stress of the poem develops the point of view has perhaps changed. Certainly the referent of "enough" appears to modify in the last stanza—it is now the naturalness of man, the instinctiveness in him which cannot be hurt by his emotions. Yet the modifications are easy enough to follow and do not disturb the poem's comparatively simple idea. The tone of the poem seems to ask to be understood in the same cerebral way, but almost as if Thomas felt how uncertain and indefinite his attempt at this kind of explication was, he rounds it off with two lines which, though startlingly inconsequential, do give a sudden vigorous jerk to the poem's ending. What they mean in the context of the poem is another matter: it is tempting to suppose that their vigour is their function and that the matter ends there. Perhaps the poet is stressing again how little words, poetry, can give: perhaps the final line should be followed out exactly—crumbs of consolation; a place to rest and also to store strength and experience; a voluntary dedication or servitude which may finally be (by the association of halter with hanging) an instrument of death and despair. These are what words may bring. But I have no confidence that the reader is intended to pursue these crossword clues of association: they may be simply misleading, and my tentative exegesis of the poem may bear no relation to the impression other readers may get from it.

The uncertainty here is crucial, because it is the result of Thomas's eclectic employment of language. When the poetry does not succeed in synthesising these employments, and imposing its own absolute illusion of confidence, the reader simply does not know what to do. Is he to receive a general impression, as from a Shelley lyric? Or is he to pursue all the implications of language as meticulously as he would in a poem by Pope or Donne? Both these kinds of poetry have their own confidence, their own ability to carry the reader with them, but an apparent hesitation between them in the poet makes for a complete bewilderment in the reader.

I think we must conclude that on these grounds "Out of the sighs" does not come off as a poem, not because it sets too difficult a task to the reader (for as we have seen the emergent idea seems simple enough) but because it leaves him in doubt about the way to read it. Many instances of this, in poems or in parts of poems, can be found in Thomas. In the poem "I, in my intricate image" we are again confronted with an idea, almost a conceit, in the first line of the poem,

> I, in my intricate image, stride on two levels,

but in the ensuing stanzas, despite the references to "two," "twin," and so on, we cast about helplessly for a coherent development of this idea—

> Forged in man's minerals, the brassy orator
> Laying my ghost in metal,
> The scales of this twin world tread on the double,
> My half ghost in armour hold hard in death's corridor,
> To my man-iron sidle.
>
> Beginning with doom in the bulb, the spring unravels,
> Bright as her spinning-wheels, the colic season
> Worked on a world of petals;
> She threads off the sap and needles, blood and bubble
> Casts to the pine roots, raising man like a mountain
> Out of the naked entrail.
>
> Beginning with doom in the ghost, and the springing marvels,
> Image of images, my metal phantom
> Forcing forth through the harebell,
> My man of leaves and the bronze root, mortal, unmortal,
> I, in my fusion of rose and male motion,
> Create this twin miracle.

"Tread," "hold," and "sidle" must all have the same relation to the sentence of the first stanza as verbs—"my half-ghost in armour holds hard in death's corridor to my man-iron, and sidles (towards it)" would presumably be the grammatical sense rendering. It is difficult to see why the sentence should be malformed, and why the two appearances of the poet should both be armour-clad, man in iron and ghost in iron. The images then change abruptly to that thick physical vision of spring rising in man and nature which is

one of Thomas's obsessions. At the end of stanza three we look in
vain for a connection between the restatement of this "twin-ness"
theme—now seen as a "fusion of rose and male motion," and the
original image of man and ghost in armour. Further images follow,
and in the last stanza of the first section of the poem the armoured
couple are seen as invalids in a sanatorium,

> Intricate manhood of ending, the invalid rivals,
> Voyaging clockwise off the symboled harbour,
> Finding the water final,
> On the consumptives' terrace taking their two farewells,
> Sail on the level, the departing adventure,
> To the sea-blown arrival.

"On the consumptives' terrace taking their two farewells" might
almost be a line from Auden, but the image of sickness and departure is bewilderingly unlike what has gone before. It hints at a
quite different and more accurately controlled image world, like
an equally surprising line in the poem "On no work of words."

> To surrender now is to pay the expensive ogre twice.

"Expensive ogre," "invalid rivals," indicate briefly an ordered
system of metaphor unlike Thomas's own. He is as eclectic in his
images as in his words, and quite often they have a literary, as opposed to a personal and individual, origin. His frequent use of the
phrase "Death's Feather," for example, though it no doubt refers
to the custom of holding a feather to the lips of the dying to see if
they still breathe, may also derive from a recollection, I think, of
the lines in T. S. Eliot's poem "A Song for Simeon."

> My life is light, waiting for the death wind,
> Like a feather on the back of my hand.

All this does not make the reader's task any easier. In "Out of
the sighs" the poet seemed to be reaching towards an idea that
could be expressed in fairly simple language: In "I, in my intricate
image" he resigns the poem to a welter of images, none of which
exercises any authority over its neighbours.

> My images stalk the trees and the slant sap's tunnel,
> No tread more perilous, . . .

In this poem, too, the difficulties do not succeed in resolving themselves. The assistance in the composition of harmony that a master-

image would give is expressly rejected by Thomas, and this is perhaps the moment to give his own views on the subject, as they were very illuminatingly set forth to Henry Treece.

> It consciously is not my method to move concentrically round a central image. . . . A poem by myself *needs* a host of images . . . I make one image—though "make" is not the word; I let, perhaps, an image be "made" emotionally in me and then apply to it what intellectual and critical forces I possess—let it breed another, let that image contradict the first, make, out of the third image born out of the other two together, a fourth contradictory image, and let them all, within my imposed formal limits, conflict. Each image holds within it the seed of its own destruction, and my dialectical method, as I understand it, is a constant building up and breaking down of the images that come out of the central seed, which is itself destructive and constructive at the same time. . . . I do not want a poem of mine to be, nor can it be, a circular piece of experience placed nearly outside the living stream of time from which it came; a poem of mine is, or should be, a water-tight section of the stream that is flowing all ways, all warring images within it should be reconciled for that small stop of time.[2]

Two things in this account are of particular interest to us. First, the concept of warring and contradictory images, by which I take it that Thomas means images not only in conflict with each other but of a different kind from each other. As described the process has a kind of impressive formality about it, like Hegel's triadic dance, but one cannot help wondering if it does not sound more convincing in theory than it may work out in practice. Secondly, the avowed absence of retrospection: "a circular piece of experience placed nearly outside the living stream of time from which it came" would be an accurate enough description of Wordsworth's poetic method. Thomas, on the contrary, wants to achieve the equivalent of the "stream of consciousness" in prose fiction, to give the feeling of words rising instantaneously from the lapse and flow of consciousness. There is in fact a direct connection between time and language as Thomas conceives them; instead of following, and as it were making a retrospective comment on the shapelessness of consciousness, Thomas's language attempts to be part of the flow. Not that this implies facility: changing the metaphor completely in another comment on his poetry, he speaks of it as "not flowing"

[2] Henry Treece, *Dylan Thomas* (London: Ernest Benn, 1956), p. 37.

but rather "hewed out" from the intractable material of his mind. The implied admission that the poem, though it may appear to be "a watertight section" from the flux of time, is really composed as laboriously as the poetry of any more conventional craftsman, shows how difficult a task Thomas has set himself in "making a momentary peace with the images at the correct moment." Such a peace does not occur in the inchoate surge of thought and feeling inside the mind: it must be imposed from without, while at the same time the illusion of time's flow in the receptive mind must be retained, and it is not surprising that the trick of this does not always come off.

When it does, we are no more conscious of the conflict of disparate images which—so Thomas tells us—have gone to make the poem, than we are when we read any other kind of Romantic poem—*Kubla Khan* for example. Moreover, Thomas is often at his most successful when he is as much *outside* the poem as we are —when he is *telling* us what he is feeling and doing, instead of obscurely *doing* it; when, in fact, the poet seems at a conventional remove from his poem, like the craftsman from his material. It is for this reason that the early poem "Especially when the October wind" is one of the finest of Thomas's achievements. The "outsideness" here is most marked, and it takes the form of the poet's identifying the languages he uses with the objects he so vividly perceives. A kind of external convention is produced, in which the poet formally attaches the terminology of language—"Vowelled," "wordy," "syllabic," "signature," "speeches," "signs"—to the world of nature —water, women, birds, and so forth.

> Shut, too, in a tower of words, I mark
> On the horizon walking like the trees
> The wordy shapes of women, and the rows
> Of the star-gestured children in the park.
> Some let me make you of the vowelled beeches,
> Some of the oaken voices, from the roots
> Of many a thorny shire tell you notes,
> Some let me make you of the water's speeches.
>
> Behind a pot of ferns the wagging clock
> Tells me the hour's word, the neural meaning
> Flies on the shafted disk, declaims the morning
> And tells the windy weather in the cock.
> Some let me make you of the meadow's signs;

The signal grass that tells me all I know
Breaks with the wormy winter through the eye.
Some let me tell you of the raven's sins.

Especially when the October wind
(Some let me make you of autumnal spells,
The spider-tongued and the loud hill of Wales)
With fists of turnips punishes the land,
Some let me make you of the heartless words.
The heart is drained that, spelling in the scurry
Of chemic blood, warned of the coming fury.
By the sea's side hear the dark-vowelled birds.

With the aid of this convention—and though brilliantly idiosyn-
cratic it is really as straightforward as Yeats's calculated terseness or
Wordsworth's impressionistic lucidity of diction—Thomas does
achieve in these early poems an objective identification of his subject matter with the language in which he describes it. The convention is, I think, the key to these poems' success and originality of
impact. It is an unadmitted convention: it has nothing to do with
the dialectical war and peace of images in which, as we have seen,
Thomas later came to envisage the theoretic process of a poem. But
it has much to do with the gap between word as thing and word
as sign, and the still greater gap between language and the actuality of blood, growth, procreation—the obsessional subject-matter of
the poems. It is a method of bridging—or appearing to bridge—
these gaps, and its operation has the supreme advantages of clarity
and order—we see what is happening and are compelled by it.
There is no doubt here, as there is elsewhere in Thomas, about how
we are to react to this phraseology: it is self-explanatory, and gives
the impression—common in more conventional poems that come
off—that the poem is in some way a *prelude* to the poetic experience which it will arouse in the reader: it carries us along with it,
moved but unquestioning, to its close, and it is then we begin to
wonder about the nature of the words that have been said to us,
and to analyse them. While the poet is talking we listen: when he
has finished we ask questions. It is this order of response which is
lacking when Thomas tries to telescope the process, and to make
his experience as poet in some way coexistent with our experience
as reader. In poems like "Out of the sighs" and "I, in my intricate
image," the linguistic stages of examination, narration, and response are jumbled together—our groping reaction is uncomforta-

bly simultaneous with Thomas's groping approach, and we feel that the attempt to jump the gaps of language and feeling has not succeeded. The attempt there seems fundamentally unaesthetic and doomed to failure. We might compare it with Thomas's use of the word "petrol" in the line

> Turning a petrol face blind to the enemy

which I have already commented on. If I am right in supposing that "petrol" is there purely because its inertness as a word corresponds to the meaningless inertia of death—Thomas might presumably have said "apron" or "bamboo" or "income" to get the same effect, if those words happened to possess a comparable euphony— the whole aesthetic function of language as a search within formal limits and rules, for the right, the nicely indicative word, is threatened with breakdown. Similarly, if the mental stages underlying the formulation and response to language—the sequence of coherence—is ignored, it is difficult to see why words should be used at all. The logical end would be Mallarmé's sheet of blank paper, or the self-imposed silence of the more extreme surrealists.

When Thomas's desire to bring words and experience closer together is successful, therefore, it succeeds through the use of a convention in no way different from the type of convention of which poets have always made use. He speaks of words, blood, women, in the same breath, and with the same almost terrifyingly intense awareness of their *existence*. It is an awareness of everything as vocal, as talking to him as he talks himself. "The spider-*tongued*, and the *loud* hill of Wales." For Thomas, not only is seeing a language, as Coleridge remarked: *being* is a language too. It is a highly personal use of a metaphor—the pathetic fallacy Ruskin called it— which poetry has always possessed. Skies have always wept in poetry, trees moaned, blood been eloquent. But Thomas's apprehension of this metaphor is far more acute and ordered than that of any previous poet. He is conscious of language as

> the voice that, like a voice of hunger,
> Itched in the noise of wind and sun.

In the poem "I fellowed sleep" he writes:

> Then all the matter of the living air
> Raised up a voice, and, climbing on the words,
> I spelt my vision with a hand and hair. . . .

The senses are compressed and interchanged—*matter* of the air, a voice *itching*, thoughts *smell* in the rain. This synaesthesia gives the abstractness of thought and language the almost overpowering reality of Thomas's physical apprehensions like

> Some dead undid their bushy jaws,
> And bags of blood let out their flies,

or

> The bagpipe-breasted ladies in the deadweed
> Blew out the blood gauze through the wound of manwax.

He speaks of the "supper and knives of a mood," and in the later poems the convention is still kept up, with phrases like "oyster vowels," "meat of a fable," "wick of words." Thomas is haunted by the indivisibility of mind and matter. The throat is where

> Words and water make a mixture
> Unfailing till the blood run foul . . .

and the brain, he says,

> was celled and soldered in the thought
> Before the pitch was forking to a sun.

The "shapes of thoughts"—a perfect phrase for Thomas's use of words—and the "declension of the flesh" constitute a kind of extended organic metaphor in Thomas's poetry. "Man be my metaphor" he ends one poem, and he tries to convey that the speaking function of man, so far from being a civilised accomplishment and overlay, is as deep and mysterious as his unconscious instincts. Even the sea does not elude the language metaphor in which Thomas invests creation and gives it order. In a note about his poems—and his prose vocabulary has all the characteristics of his poetry—he speaks of the "unparagraphed" sea.

Of course this metaphoric structure is not the explanation of the poetry's power—many other factors are involved as well. Most notable of these is Thomas's skill in juxtaposing sounds, vowels and consonants, to produce an almost physical impact. His oral vigour is amazing—one would scarcely believe that English was capable of it—and depends for its complete effect upon an un-English fullness of articulation, the kind of articulation which Thomas gave to his reading. Consider the movement of "some dead undid their bushy

jaws," and the X and Z sounds between the long U's in "Blew out
the blood gauze through the wound of manwax."

> And I am dumb to mouth unto my veins
> How at the mountain spring the same mouth sucks.

The effectiveness of sound as a part of sense does not need to be
laboured. It is a traditional part, a function of language as "thing,"
which has always been used as an adjunct to poetic meaning, and
is quite different from the attempt, which Thomas sometimes seems
to be making, to get sound and referential pointlessness to carry
language closer to mood and feeling. His poetry, as in the examples
just quoted, often both means and sounds physically: the sensation
is that we are being assaulted by some means other than words. And
this again shows how powerful is the double use of language in his
poetry. If I read the sentence: "He came at her with a knife," I may
shrink from the scene conjured up by its meaning, if I am a sensitive person, but this reaction will be caused by the words as indica-
tors, not as things. Even an apparently strenuous couplet of Auden's,

> And mobilise the powerful forces latent
> In the infected sinus and the eyes of stoats . . .

though it seems at first to resemble Thomas in its insistence on
physical detail, will be found, I think, to operate almost entirely
referentially if we compare it to Thomas's

> her threadbare
> Whisper in a damp word, her wits drilled hollow,
> Her fist of a face died clenched on a round pain,

or

> The swing of milk was tufted in the pap,

where the "thinginess" of language seems to flourish alongside its
sense, and is deliberately courted as an accessory to physical references. In this, as in so much else, Thomas has revived rather than
invented. We find the effect in Pope,

> . . . Alum styptics with contracting power
> Shrink his thin essence like a shrivelled flower—

where the physical thinness of the words is a part of their total meaning, and—with a fullness of vowels like Thomas's own—in Keats,

> Then glut thy sorrow on a morning rose,
> Or on the wealth of globed peonies. . . .

I return to insist on the importance in Thomas's poetry of this dual function of language, because the peculiar use he has made of it will perhaps be his chief claim to distinction. At a time when the language of poetry has seemed to be in danger of being pulled apart between the meaningless exuberance of surrealism on the one hand, and the self-conscious precision of poets influenced by positivistic theory on the other, he has achieved a balance between the two, in his best poems, while retaining—and even drawing our attention to —the separateness of both. It is because of this separateness that his poetry does not lend itself to analysis in terms of its content. Indeed we can go so far as to say that whenever such analysis is possible, and seems desirable, the poem has not been a success. A prose paraphrase, such as those attempted by Julian Symons, and made the basis of an adverse verdict on the poems, is clearly no sort of critical lever at all. Except on rare occasions—as in "Out of the sighs" and "The hand that signed the paper"—even an attempt to say what Thomas's subject is only leads to misunderstanding and to a shrinking of the poem's true dimension.

This is not to say that any criticism of the poetry must be of a purely negative kind, though I think that indication of the types of linguistic experience we encounter in his work, and of how we may best enjoy them, remains the most constructive critical approach. One more positive evaluation that may be made, however—and this is also closely bound up with his linguistic practice—is of the way in which he achieves the effect of compression in time, the physical reality of "in my beginning is my end" which of all Thomas's special apprehensions is the one most powerfully conceived and carried out. We must remember here our earlier remarks on his symbolism. Thomas's awareness is never expressed "symbolically" when it conveys this prehension, but always with absolute literalness: he himself said that he wished his poetry to be taken literally, and at its best—as when this kind of awareness is involved—it always can be. There is no gap—no intellectually sensible gap that is—between our grasping of the words and our deduction of what they are supposed to stand for. It is this gap which is the nemesis of so much poetic symbolism, and when it does not occur it is perfectly accurate to speak of the poem or part of the poem as "literal." In this sense Blake's poem "O Rose Thou art Sick," is literal, and so is Thomas's "Twenty-four years."

> Twenty-four years remind the tears of my eyes.
> (Bury the dead for fear that they walk to the grave in labour.)
> In the groin of the natural doorway I crouched like a tailor
> Sewing a shroud for a journey
> By the light of the meat-eating sun.
> Dressed to die, the sensual strut begun,
> With my red veins full of money,
> In the final direction of the elementary town
> I advance for as long as forever is.

We do not need to ask what this poem is *about*. It means what it says, and the line "In the groin of the natural doorway I crouched like a tailor" does not refer to the concept of birth any more than Blake's "Invisible worm that flies in the night, in the howling storm" refers to an abstract idea of evil, energy, the male principle, etc. A symbol in poetry, if it works, might be defined as a literal statement which can be apprehended so clearly that this very shock of apprehension conveys other possibilities of meaning. We can apprehend it, but not explain it, for, in the words of Wittgenstein, "that which expresses *itself* in language we cannot express by language." The secret of the symbol's power to set the mind at work is its initial confidence, vigour, and absorption in itself. This is why the literalness of a fairy story often seems to mean more than it says, or lines like,

> The Queen was dressed in scarlet
> Her merry maids all in green—

Or Thomas's own,

> And there this night I walk in the white giant's thigh.

Thomas's own comment on a poem of his criticising Edith Sitwell's analysis of some lines in it, is very illuminating.

> Altarwise by owl-light in the half-way house
> The gentleman lay graveward with his furies;
> Abaddon in the hangnail cracked from Adam,
> And, from his fork, a dog among the fairies,

> The atlas-eater with a jaw for news,
> Bit out the mandrake with tomorrow's scream.

Of the last two lines Edith Sitwell commented: "they refer to the violent speed and the sensation-loving, horror-loving craze of modern life." Thomas remarked that this was very vague. "She doesn't take the literal meaning: that a world-devouring ghost creature bit out the horror of tomorrow from a gentlemen's loins." This is certainly literal and graphic enough, but the thought strikes us, could not Edith Sitwell's interpretation follow from the literal meaning? Isn't her meaning legitimate for her, and for anyone else whose feelings and preoccupations happen to be ignited in the same way by the lines? Does an insistence on literal meaning, in fact, save us from the ensuing welter of subjective reactions? The answer is, perhaps, that a literalness of the graphic and absolute kind indicated by Thomas (and Edith Sitwell does seem to have ignored the castration image that the syntax uncompromisingly insists on) should preclude any vagueness of response, such as ideas about the speed of modern life, etc. A graphic, unambiguous statement should never produce a vague suggestion. But the opposite of vague here is not clearly formulated. As Arthur Symons wrote in his essay on Maeterlinck: "All art hates the vague; not the *mysterious,* but the vague: two opposites very commonly confused." Whatever we get from Thomas's lines will not be easy to express, but it will, or should, be controlled by the literal violence of his words which pin down our response to certain kinds of actuality. The reason why poetic symbols (as can be seen in the case of Yeats) are often vague and dreamy is because there is less discrepancy between the images and the impressions we get from them; the creator's unconscious reasoning seems to be: impressions from poetry are inchoate, therefore let the words and sentences that produce them be the same. "O world! O life! O time!"—Shelley's poem invites the vaguest and most ethereal possible response. But as we have said, the inchoate is not necessarily vague, nor is it abstract. The movement in the mind of words like "fork," "jaw," "scream," "bit," is sufficiently forcible to prevent the journey from the words themselves to parallel abstractions about them. We are back here at the linguistic problem with which we started: the alternative (admittedly an oversimplified one) of stopping at the words or penetrating into the thought behind them. If the thought can only appear, like Edith Sitwell's version of it, at an unwarrantable remove from the words, we are unwise to seek for it. *Search* for Thomas's meaning is a dangerous process; we may have to read a passage carefully to discover its literal meaning, but, once discovered, there should be no further conscious search for a concealed significance; Thomas's own gloss on the extract gives an indication of how the literal meaning can be followed up rather than interpreted. "The mouth of the creature (the Atlas-eater) can taste already the horror that is not yet come, or can sense its coming, can thrust its tongue into news that has not yet been made, can savour the enormity of the progeny before the seed stirs, can realise the crumbling of dead flesh before the opening of the womb that delivers the flesh to tomorrow."

The lines, in fact, show Thomas's obsessional theme, the telescoping of existence—"Time held me green and dying." And we shall find it whenever we look behind the words. That is why we may feel a sense of disappointment and limitation if we are continually looking for an idea, and may prefer—as Edith Sitwell evidently preferred—to suppose that Thomas is making some kind of poetic comment, about "modern life." Another critic's interpretation of the first stanza of "When, like a running grave"—

> When, like a running grave, time tracks you down,
> Your calm and cuddled is a scythe of hairs,
> Love in her gear is slowly through the house,
> Up naked stairs, a turtle in a hearse,
> Hauled to the dome,

—suggests that the image of the dead turtle-dove taken to the skull means "when love is intellectualised." Apart from the fact that turtle-dove, though poetic, receives no warrant in the text—the grotesque side of Thomas and the word "haul" indicate a more conventional turtle—the idea of "intellectualising" is a concept at an immense distance from the words: we cannot move from the words towards such a hypothetical idea at the back of them without doing violence to the actuality of the poem. Granted that the image is puzzling, it seems likely that once again the subject is the coincidence in time of birth, love, and death—the image of going upstairs is used more than once in Thomas to indicate this process, as in "The Conversation of Prayer,"

> . . . the man on the stairs
> Who climbs to his dying love in her high room . . .
> And mark the dark eyed wave, through the eyes of sleep,
> Dragging him up the stairs to one who lies dead.

And the reference to skulls in the later stanzas of "When, like a running grave" indicates the death aspect of the theme traditionally enough ("to this favour must she come") without any need to suppose that Thomas is concealing with images *ideas* about the nature of love.

None the less, the poet himself is partly to blame. If we are confused and baffled by a literal reading, it is difficult not to cast about for some explanation or "message" contained in the poem. Literalness is often not forcible enough for us to recognise its implications without trying to interpret it. Thus Professor Olson suggests that "Ballad of the Long-legged Bait" "deals with the possibility of salvation through mortification of the flesh." The implication is that Thomas is writing a mediaeval allegory, a kind of *Piers Ploughman*, or at least a poem with the moral structure of *The Ancient Mariner*, whereas the comparison should rather be with, say, Rimbaud's "Bateau Ivre"—both poems are a vision of life rather than the treatment of a problem in life. Where the symbolic is concerned, and in Thomas in particular, energy can often act as a kind of substitute for clarity. It was Yeats who first employed symbols in English in the energetic style, and Thomas's most successful poems display the same characteristic. In "Twenty-four years," for example, the energy of the poem carries us through without a halt. The only word which might give us pause is "elementary," where we should expect "elemental," but the reason for it is partly euphony, to avoid a repetition of the "al"-sound two lines back; and partly —one imagines—to get the shock effect of peeling off the normal associations of a commonplace word to reveal its basic meaning. The compressed violence of the second line is contextual for Thomas: he echoes it infrequently—"In the groin's endless coil a man is tangled"—and "my father's ghost is climbing in the rain," in phrases like "dressed to die," and in "After the funeral"—

> . . . a desolate boy who slits his throat
> In the dark of the coffin and sheds dry leaves.

It is at these moments, too, that the elevated and rhapsodic movement and tone, which the Welsh preachers and their audiences call *Hwyll*, is most marked. This uplifted but natural eloquence is scarcely heard at all today in English poetry—the kinds of self-consciousness which we have noticed in Eliot and Auden are an effective deterrent to it—and the movement of "After the funeral," with its unfaltering and yet disciplined exaltation, sends us back to the tradition of *Lycidas* and Spenser's *Daphnaida*.

A criticism often made about Dylan Thomas is that he did not develop, that his subject matter is purely himself, and that once he had brought out "from darkness to light" the obscure matter which obsessed him, his poetic potentialities were exhausted. It is true that his poems are always, broadly speaking, about the same thing, and the most striking difference between his early and his later poems is the way in which what had been groping and shapeless, an exploratory movement continued from one poem to the next, takes on a closed and almost geometrical completeness of form. "From love's first fever to her plague" has the same preoccupation with the unity of our bodily experiences in time—birth, copulation, death—as a late poem, "The Conversation of Prayer." But the later poem, with its delicately handled scheme of inner rhymes, is intent on establishing an already known fact by technical means, by an aesthetic pattern, almost as the mood of Owen's "Strange Meeting" or Auden's "Pleasure Island" is determined by these means, while in the early poem the apprehension in the poet's mind has still to be explored and given provisional shape. But this shift from exploration to aesthetic presentation does not make "The Conversation of Prayer" any weaker than its predecessor: on the contrary, the later poem seems to me in every way better. To suppose that when a poet does not know what he wants to say before he begins writing the poem must necessarily be more compelling than when he does, is a dangerously absurd criterion; but in the case of Thomas it has often been implied. What is undoubtedly true of both poems is that they cover, each in its different way, the whole poetic experience of their author. There is nothing left over. No development of *ideas* can follow from them, just as it cannot follow from Sweeney's vision of life—

> That's all the facts when you come to brass tacks:
> Birth, and copulation, and death.

But Sweeney reflects his author's horror at these "facts," from which some kind of release must be found, which demand some sort of higher explanation; while for Thomas their simple existence is enough for poetry.

Nor, in Thomas's later work, is their existence apprehended only in the individual, in the poet himself. It might seem that his world was necessarily an enclosed one, a world of intuitions about the imprisoned self which could be shared between writer and reader but is not capable of demonstration in terms of the communal nature of man. *Under Milk Wood* shows that this is not the case. As Auden in *The Age of Anxiety* gives us a drama not of social relationships but of the interrelated fantasy life of four individuals, so Thomas presents society in terms of a day in a Welsh village, a day which is also a lifetime. His invariable vision, the jumble of death and life, is extroverted into a frieze of figures, young and old, male and female. The women gossip round the pump.

> Same as ever. Who's having a baby, who blacked whose eye, seen Polly Garter giving her belly an airing, there should be a law, seen Mrs Beynon's new mauve jumper, it's her old grey jumper dyed, who's dead, who's dying, there's a lovely day, oh the cost of soapflakes!

Polly Garter addresses her baby.

> You're looking up at me now. I know what you're thinking, you poor little milky creature. You're thinking, you're no better than you should be, Polly, and that's good enough for me. Oh, isn't life a terrible thing, thank God?

The drowned speak to Captain Cat, the old seaman, who sails back into the past "through the voyages of his tears."

> How's it above? Is there rum and laverbread? Bosoms and robins? . . . Fighting and Onions? . . . Washing on the line? And old girls in the snug? Who milks the cows in Maesgwyn? When she smiles, is there dimples? What's the smell of parsley?

In his imagination Mr Edwards addresses impassioned pleas to his beloved.

> I am a draper mad with love. I love you more than all the flannelette and calico, candlewick, dimity, crash and merino, tussore, cretonne, crepon, muslin, poplin, ticking and twill in the whole Cloth Hall of the world. I have come to take you away to my Emporium on the hill, where the change hums on wires. Throw away your little bedsocks and your Welsh wool knitted jacket, I will warm the sheets like an electric toaster, I will lie by your side like the Sunday roast.

As the second quotation shows, Thomas does not avoid (indeed it is probably not his purpose to avoid) a certain coarsening here of the vitality which wells up so strangely in his poems. "Isn't life a terrible thing, thank God" might indeed be a summing-up of the impression that his poety leaves with us, but here it is too much a short cut, too arch an approximation, which reminds us uncomfortably of the "wind on the heath, brother," Chesterton and Belloc style of affirmation. But though *Under Milk Wood* was intended specifically for a wireless audience such overt forcing of the atmosphere does not often occur: on the whole the play carries through its conviction of reality successfully by means of its separate characters. In becoming more "popular" and giving his individual vision a social basis, Thomas puts himself in the tradition of vivid and colloquial fantasy which runs from Shakespeare and Congreve through Dickens to James Joyce, and he uses this tradition in the best sense, without sacrificing any of his own individuality. Mr Pugh, dreaming of poisoning his wife, is a figure who takes his place in an august line of English fantastics, but he is also pure Thomas.

> Alone in the hissing laboratory of his wishes, Mr Pugh minces among bad vats and jeroboams, tiptoes through spinneys of murdering herbs, agony dancing in his crucibles, and mixes especially for Mrs Pugh a venomous porridge unknown to toxicologists which will scald and viper through her until her ears fall off like figs, her toes grow big and black as balloons, and steam comes screaming out of her navel.

There are the same syllabic contrasts and concealed rhymes, but the language has become more consistently exact, its combination of "thing" and reference more orthodox, without losing any of its vigour. It is done as engagingly as Rosetta's daydreams in *The Age of Anxiety* but with an undernote of physical reality and violence as graphic as the ghost's description of the poisoning in *Hamlet*. Phrases like "Samson-syrup-gold-maned,"—'she sleeps very dulcet in a cove of wool"—cows as "summerbreathed slaves walking delicately to the farm"—equally announce the fact that Thomas seems to have returned to the fold of conventional aesthetic language.

We can almost equate, then, Thomas's inclusion of society in his poetic vision with a return to tradition. If he had lived, his poetry might have continued to develop along the lines suggested by the "public" subject of *Under Milk Wood*. The figure of Polly Garter in particular (we may remember Arnold's depression at the name and the idea of the accused woman Wragg) suggests that Thomas might have been able to create characters drawn from common life but living and breathing in poetry, instead of the characters with a poetic halo stuck artificially round them who inhabit contemporary poetic drama. Beginning in himself, Thomas's poetic apprehension, so absolute and so homogeneous, was beginning to turn outwards into the world of other human beings, seen as individuals going about their concerns. He had no need to create a world of myth out of this real world as did the other poets whom we have studied: its existence, like his own existence, would have been enough. He would have seen Man, as he had seen himself, "up to his head in his blood," and—for that very reason—also up to his head in a world of poetry.

Dylan Thomas

by Karl Shapiro

The death of Dylan Thomas in 1953 was the cause of the most singular demonstration of suffering in modern literary history. One searches the memory in vain for any parallel to it. At thirty-nine Thomas had endeared himself to the literary youth of England and America, to most of the poets who were his contemporaries, and to many who were his elders; he was the master of a public which he himself had brought out of nothingness; he was the idol of writers of every description and the darling of the press. (The Press scented him early and nosed him to the grave.) Critics had already told how Thomas became the first poet who was both popular and obscure. In an age when poets are supposed to be born old, everyone looked upon Thomas as the last of the young poets. When he died, it was as if there would never be any more youth in the world. Or so it seemed in the frenzy of his year-long funeral, a funeral which, like one of Thomas's own poems, turned slowly into a satanic celebration and a literary institution.

When Yeats and Valéry died, old and wise and untouchable, there were held, so to speak, the grand state funerals. It was Civilization itself that mourned. When Thomas died, a poet wrote wildly how, to get him up in the morning, he plugged Thomas's mouth with a bottle of beer—"this wonderful baby." All the naughty stories were on everybody's lips; all the wrong things began to be said, and the right things in the wrong way. Someone quoted bitterly: Kill him, he's a poet! and this childishness was the signal for a verbal massacre of the bourgeoisie, reminiscent of the early decades of our century.

The death of a young poet inflicts a psychic wound upon the

world and is the cause among poets themselves of frightening babbling and soothsaying. Such doings may be likened to a witches'
Sabbath, and some have seen in these morbid celebrations the very
coming-to-life of Thomas's poems. It is his death as an occasion for
literary and psychological insurrection that must interest us today,
if we are to understand the meaning of Thomas's poetry and the significance his contemporaries have given it. It is one thing to analyze
and interpret poetry and keep it all in a book; it is another to
watch that poetry enter an audience and melt it to a single mind. I
want to speak about the second thing, the live thing, the thing that
touched the raw nerve of the world and that keeps us singing with
pain. The poetry of Thomas is full of the deepest pain; there are
few moments of relief. What is the secret of his pain-filled audience? How are we to place Thomas among the famous impersonal
poets of our time, when this one is so personal, so intimate and so
profoundly grieved? Thomas was the first modern romantic you
could put your finger on, the first whose journeys and itineraries
became part of his own mythology, the first who offered himself up
as a public, not a private, sacrifice. Hence the piercing sacrificial
note in his poetry, the uncontainable voice, the drifting, almost
ectoplasmic character of the man, the desperate clinging to a few
drifting spars of literary convention. Hence, too, the universal acclaim for his lyricism, and the mistaken desire to make him an heir
to Bohemia or to the high Symbolist tradition.

Writers said of Thomas that he was the greatest lyricist of our
time. The saying became a platitude. It was unquestionably true,
but what did the word mean? It meant that, in contrast to the epic
pretensions of many of the leading modern poets, he was the only
one who could be called a singer. To call him the best lyric poet of
our time was to pay him the highest, the only compliment. Nearly
everyone paid him this splendid compliment and everyone knew its
implications. Few realized, however, that this compliment marked
a turning point in poetry.

During his life there were also the armed camps who made him
honorary revolutionary general; and we cannot be sure Thomas re-
fused the homemade epaulets of these border patrols. I rather think
he was proud to be taken in. Who were these people? First there
was the remnant of Bohemia. These are people who exist in the
belief that everyone is dead except themselves. I saw one of these

poets lately; he had just come from England and he informed me casually that everyone in England is dead. To change the subject I asked him if he was glad to be home; but it turned out that everyone in America is also dead. Among these poets there is a sincere belief in the death of our world, and it is curious to speculate upon their adoption of Thomas as a leader and a patron saint. In the same way nearly all of Thomas's followers have spoken of him as a Symbolist. The Symbolists praise the love of death as the highest order of poetic knowledge. "Bohemian" and Symbolist are never far apart.

All the same, this theory of posthumous vitality seems to make sense when we speak of Thomas. How much did Thomas subscribe to official Symbolism? Just enough to provide ammunition for those people. How much did he love death as his major symbol? As much as any poet in the English language. These factions have a claim on Thomas which we cannot contradict.

Thomas is in somewhat the relation to modern poetry that Hopkins was to the Victorians—a lone wolf. Thomas resisted the literary traditionalism of the Eliot school; he wanted no part of it. Poetry to him was not a civilizing maneuver, a replanting of the gardens; it was a holocaust, a sowing of the wind. And we cannot compare Thomas, say, with Auden, because they are different in kind. Thomas's antithesis to Auden, as to Eliot, is significant. Thomas grew up in a generation which had lost every kind of cultural leadership. The poets who began to write during the Depression, which was worse in Wales than in America, were deprived of every traditional ideal. The favorite poem of this generation was Yeats's "The Second Coming." Yeats's poems gave to a generation of prematurely wise young poets an apocalypse, a vision of Antichrist and a vision of the downfall of civilization. The theatricality of the Yeats poem was a great convenience to a poet like Thomas who, having nothing of true philosophical or religious substance to fall back upon, could grasp this straw. The acknowledged precedence of Yeats in modern English literature—in world literature perhaps—has been a makeshift consolation to all modern poets. Yeats, with his cruel forcing of the imagination, his jimmying of the spirit, is a heroic figure in modern poetry. Yet he belongs to the past, with all its claptrap of history and myth. Thomas's poetry was born out of the bankruptcy of the Yeats-Pound-Eliot "tradition" and all it stood for. It was born out of the revulsion against the book-poetry of Auden and the system-mongering of the social revolutionaries. Thomas's poetry was orphaned from the start.

Thomas suffers from the waifishness imposed upon his generation. The so-called Apocalyptic poets, which he was supposed to be a member of, never existed. Nor is he one of the Metaphysical school. One can see that he plays around with copying the superficies of Vaughan and Herbert and Traherne and maybe David ap Gwilym (who in English is not much better than James Whitcomb Riley) and Yeats and Hopkins. But Thomas was outside the orbit of the English poets and maybe the Welsh. He was antitradition by nature, by place, by inclination. Certainly Thomas's grisly love for America can also be seen in this light; America is the untraditional place, the Romantic country par excellence.

Thomas's technique is deceptive. When you look at it casually you think it is nothing. The meter is banal. It is no better and no worse than that of dozens of other poets his age. There is no invention and a great deal of imitation. There is no theory. But despite his lack of originality, the impress of Thomas's idiom on present-day English poetry is incalculable. One critic said not many years ago that Thomas had visited a major affliction on English poetry. This was an unfriendly way of saying that Thomas had captured the young poets, which he certainly had. How did he do this? He did it through the force of emotion, with the personal idiom, a twist of the language, bending the iron of English. Once he had bent this iron his way everybody else tried it. Thomas has more imitators today than any other poet in the literature. Whether this excitement will last a year or a hundred years, no one can tell. But it is a real excitement.

Yet even when we examine the texture of his language we fail to find anything original, although we find something completely distinctive. It is hard to locate the distinctiveness of Thomas's idiom. There are a few tricks of word order, a way of using a sentence, a characteristic vocabulary, an obsessive repetition of phrase, and so on—things common to many lesser poets. Again, if we scrutinize his images and metaphors, which are much more impressive than the things I have mentioned, we frequently find overdevelopment, blowziness, and euphemism, on the one hand, and brilliant crystallization on the other. But no system, no poetic, no practice that adds up to anything you can hold on to. The more you examine him as a stylist the less you find.

What does this mean? It means that Thomas is a quite derivative, unoriginal, *unintellectual* poet, the entire force of whose personality and vitality is jammed into his few difficult half-intelligible poems. To talk about Thomas as a Symbolist is dishonest. Not long ago in Hollywood Aldous Huxley introduced a Stravinksy composition based on a poem of Thomas's. Huxley quoted that line of Mallarmé's which says that poets purify the dialect of the tribe. This, said Huxley, was what Thomas did. Now anybody who has read Thomas knows that he did the exact opposite: Thomas did everything in his power to obscure the dialect of the tribe—whatever that high-and-mighty expression may mean. Thomas sometimes attempted to keep people from understanding his poems (which are frequently simple, once you know the dodges). He had a horror of simplicity—or what I consider to be a fear of it. He knew little except what a man knows who has lived about forty years, and there was little he wanted to know. There is a fatal pessimism in most of his poems, offset by a few bursts of joy and exuberance. The main symbol is masculine love, driven as hard as Freud drove it. In the background is God, hard to identify but always there, a kind of God who belongs to one's parents rather than to the children, who do not quite accept Him.

I went through the *Collected Poems* recently to decide which poems I would keep if I were editing the best poems of Dylan Thomas. Out of about ninety poems I chose more than thirty which I think stand with the best poems of our time. If this seems a small number, we should remember that there are not many more poems upon which the fame of Hopkins rests; of Rimbaud; or, for that matter, of John Donne. And yet we expect a greater volume of work from such an exuberant man. Thomas's sixty poems that I would exclude are short of his mark, but they are not failures. I would like to name by name those poems which I think belong to the permanent body of our poetry—or most of them anyway: "I see the boys of summer"; "A process in the weather of the heart"; "The force that through the green fuse drives the flower"; "Especially when the October wind"; "When, like a running grave"; "Light breaks where no sun shines"; "Do you not father me"; "A grief ago"; "And death shall have no dominion"; "Then was my neophyte"; "When all my five and country senses see"; "We lying by seasand"; "It is the sinners' dust-tongued bell"; "After the funeral"; "Not from this anger"; "How shall my animal"; "Twenty-four years"; "A Refusal to Mourn"; "Poem in October"; "The Hunchback in the Park"; "Into her Lying Down Head"; "Do not go gentle"; "A Winter's Tale"; "On the Marriage of a Virgin"; "When I Woke"; "Among those Killed in the Dawn Raid"; "Fern Hill"; "In country sleep"; "Over Sir John's hill"; and "Poem on his birthday." I leave out the sonnets, which I think are forced, and the "Ballad of the Long-legged Bait," and the "Prologue," and many others. My list is probably off here and there, but I think it is the substantial list of works by which Thomas will be remembered.

The "major" poems, that is, the more pretentious poems, such as the ten sonnets (called "Altarwise by owl-light"), reveal most of what we know of Thomas's convictions and what we can call his philosophy. He believed in God and Christ, the Fall and death, the end of all things and the day of eternity. This is very conventional religion and Thomas was uncritical about it. Add to this the puritanism which runs through his whole work, and, finally, the forced optimism in the last poems such as "In country sleep" in which, although the whole sequence is unfinished, there is a recognizable affirmation of faith in life. But one feels that these matters are not of paramount importance in the poetry of Thomas. Thomas was not interested in philosophical answers. Religion, such as he knew it, was direct and natural; the symbolism of religion, as he uses it, is poetry, direct knowledge. Religion is not to be used: it is simply part of life, part of himself; it is like a tree; take it or leave it, it is there. In this sense, one might say that Thomas is more "religious" than Eliot, because Thomas has a natural religious approach to nature and to himself. The language of Thomas, not the style, is very close to that of Hopkins, not only in obvious ways, but in its very method. Hopkins, however, arrived at his method philosophically, abstractly, as well as through temperament and neurosis. Thomas, with no equipment for theorizing about the forms of nature, sought the "forms" that Hopkins did. The chief difference between the two poets in terms of their symbols is that Hopkins draws his symbology almost entirely from the God-symbol. God, in various attributes, is the chief process in Hopkins's view of the world. Sex is the chief process in Thomas's view of the world.

Thomas's idea of process is important. The term itself is rather mechanistic, as he uses it. He always takes the machine of energy rather than some abstraction, such as spirit or essence. Hence the concreteness of his words and images; obscurity occurs also because of the "process" of mixing the imagery of the subconscious with biological imagery, as in Hopkins. But there is also a deliberate attempt to involve the subconscious as the main process: Thomas's imagination, which is sometimes fantastic, works hard to dredge up the images of fantasy and dreams. Very often the process fails and we are left with heaps of grotesque images that add up to nothing. I would equate the process in Thomas's poetics with his rather startling views of the sexual process. Aside from those poems in which sex is simply sung, much as poets used to write what are called love poems, there are those poems in which sex is used as the instrument of belief and knowledge. Using the cliché of modern literature that everyone is sick and the whole world is a hospital, Thomas wants to imply that sex will make us (or usually just him) healthy and whole again. And there are suggestions of Druidism (perhaps) and primitive fertility rites, apparently still extant in Wales, all mixed up with Henry Miller, Freud, and American street slang. But sex kills also, as Thomas says a thousand times, and he is not sure of the patient's recovery. In place of love, about which Thomas is almost always profoundly bitter, there is sex, the instrument and the physical process of love. The activity of sex, Thomas hopes in his poems, will somehow lead to love in life and in the cosmos. As he grows older, love recedes and sex becomes a nightmare, a Black Mass.

Thomas moves between sexual revulsion and sexual ecstasy, between puritanism and mysticism, between formalistic ritual (this accounts for his lack of invention) and vagueness. In his book one comes, on one page, upon a poem of comparative peace and lucidity, and on the next page upon a poem of absolute density and darkness. His dissatisfaction with his own lack of stability is reflected in his devices which tend to obscure even the simple poems; he leaves out all indications of explanation—quotation marks, punctuation, titles, connectives, whether logical or grammatical. In addition he uses every extreme device of ambiguity one can think of, from reversing the terms of a figure of speech to ellipsis to over-elaboration of images. There is no poetic behind these practices— only catch-as-catch-can technique. One is always confused in Thomas by not knowing whether he is using the microscope or the telescope; he switches from one to the other with ease and without warning. It is significant that his joyous poems, which are few, though among his best, are nearly always his simplest. Where the dominant theme of despair obtrudes, the language dives down into the depths; some of these complex poems are among the most rewarding, the richest in feeling, and the most difficult to hold to. But, beyond question, there are two minds working in Thomas, the joyous, naturally religious mind, and the disturbed, almost pathological mind of the cultural fugitive or clown. On every level of Thomas's work one notices the lack of sophistication and the split in temperament. This is his strength as well as his weakness. But it is a grave weakness because it leaves him without defense, without a bridge between himself and the world.

Thomas begins in a blind alley with the obsessive statement that birth is the beginning of death, the basic poetic statement, but one which is meaningless unless the poet can build a world between. Thomas never really departs from this statement, and his obsession with sex is only the clinical restatement of the same theme. The idealization of love, the traditional solution with most poets, good and bad, is never arrived at in Thomas. He skips into the foreign land of love and skips out again. And he is too good a poet to fake love. He doesn't feel it; he distrusts it; he doesn't believe it. He falls back on the love-process, the assault, the defeat, the shame, the despair. Over and over again he repeats the ritualistic formulas for love, always doubting its success. The process is despised because it doesn't really work. The brief introduction to the *Collected Poems* sounds a note of bravado which asserts that his poems "are written for the love of Man and in praise of God." One wishes they were; one is grateful for, and slightly surprised by, the acknowledgment to God and Man, for in the poems we find neither faith nor humanism. What we find is something that fits Thomas into the age: the satanism, the vomitous horror, the self-elected crucifixion of the artist.

In the last few years of his life Thomas was beginning to find an audience. No one, I think, was more taken aback than he at this phenomenon, because most of the poems which the audience liked had been in books for five or ten years already. Thomas was the modern poet who by his *presence* created an audience. His audience was the impossible one: a general audience for a barely understandable poet. His way of meeting this audience, at the end, was no solution for Thomas as a poet. He became a dramatist, a writer of scenarios, a producer. What he wrote in this phase was not negligible by any means; but it was probably not what he wanted and not what his audience wanted. His audience wanted the poetry; they wanted the agony of the process.

The frenzy that attended Dylan Thomas's death was a frenzy of frustration. Many times, in his stories and letters and his talk, Thomas tried to leap over this frustration into a Rabelaisian faith; but it never rang true enough. After the gaiety came the hangover, the horrible fundamentalist remorse. Yet through the obscurity of the poetry everyone could feel the scream of desperation: not a cry of desire; on the contrary, it was the opposite; it was the cry of the trapped animal; the thing wanting to be man; the man wanting to be spirit.

He is a self-limiting poet and an exasperating one. He runs beyond your reach after he has beckoned you to follow; he arouses you and then slumps into a heap. He knows, more than his readers, that he has no bridge between life and death, between self and the world. His poetry is absolutely literal (as he himself insisted all the time). But its literalness is the challenge to literature which is always significant. He is too honest to rhapsodize or to intone over the great symbols; rather he growls or rages or more often hypnotizes himself by the minute object, which he is likely to crush in his anger. Unlike Hopkins, he has no vision of nature and cannot break open the forms of nature; he cannot break open words. He focuses madly on the object, but it will not yield. He calls a weathercock a bow-and-arrow bird. Metaphor won't come and he resorts to riddle, the opposite of metaphor. A good half of his poetry is the poetry of rage; not rage at the world of society or politics or art or anything except self. He is impatient for a method and the impatience early turns into desperation, the desperation into clowning. He is another naïf, like Rimbaud, a countryman, who having left the country wanders over the face of the earth seeking a vision. He is running away from his fame, which he does not feel equal to. He is running away from the vision of self, or keeping the integrity of self by fleeing from the foci of tradition. I interpret the life and work of Thomas this way: the young poet of natural genius and expansive personality who recoils from the ritual of literary tradition and who feels himself drawn into it as into a den of iniquity. This is both the puritanism and the wisdom of Thomas. Such a man can never acquire the polish of the world which is called worldliness, and he turns to the only form of behavior, literary and otherwise, permissible both to society and to self. That is buffoonery. All the literary world loves a buffoon: the French make a saint of the clown. But folklore has it that the clown dies in the dressing room.

It is the most certain mark of Thomas's genius that he did not give way to any vision but his own, the one authentic source of knowledge he had—himself. And it is the most certain mark of his weakness that he could not shield himself from the various literary preceptors who buzzed around him. He became immobile, I think, out of pure fright. He wrote personal letters (which are now being published) apparently meant for publication, in which he adopted the modern clichés about modern life. He pretended to be horrified by the electric toaster, or maybe he really was.

The doctrinaire impersonality of our poetry demands allegiance to a Tradition, any tradition, even one you rig up for yourself. Thomas represents the extreme narrowness of the individual genius, the basic animal (one of his favorite symbols) in man. The animal to Thomas is everything and we listen because he calls it animal, not spirit or essence or potentiality or something else. It is the authentic symbol for a poet who believes in the greatness of the individual and the sacredness of the masses. It is Whitman's symbol when he says he thinks he could turn and live with animals, because they are natural and belong to nature and do not try to turn nature out of its course. They do not try to believe anything contrary to their condition.

But Thomas is drawn away from his animal; he becomes brute. And this he knows. In the brute phase of his poetry (which is the phase loved by the modernists who picked up his scent) the poetry is a relentless cutting down to the quick—surgery, butchery, and worse. And as Thomas is the one and only subject of his poems, we know what is being destroyed.

It is some of the saddest poetry we have. It leaves us finally with grief. The pathos of Thomas is that he is not diabolical, not mystical, not possessed; he has not the expansive imagination of Blake nor even the fanatical self-control of Yeats. He is the poet of genius unable to face life. Like D. H. Lawrence he is always hurling himself back into childhood and the childhood of the world. Everyone speaks of Thomas as a child. He became a child.

It is easy to dismiss him but he will not be dismissed. He was a tremendous talent who stung himself into insensibility because he could not face the obligations of intellectual life, which he mistakenly felt he must. He could not take the consequences of his own natural beliefs; and he could not temporize; there was no transition, no growth, only the two states of natural joy and intellectual despair, love of trees and fascination of the brute process. He said everything he had to say: it had little to do with wars and cities and art galleries. What he said was that man is a child thrust into the power of self, an animal becoming an angel. But becoming an angel he becomes more a beast. There is no peace, no rest, and death itself is only another kind of disgusting sex.

But something happened to his poems. Somehow the spark escaped; it leapt out of the hands of literature and set a fire. Thomas, I think, did the impossible in modern poetry. He made a jump to an audience which, we have been taught to believe, does not exist. It is an audience that understands him even when they cannot understand his poetry. It is probably the first nonfunereal poetry audience in fifty years, an audience that had been deprived of poetry by fiat. Thomas's audience bears certain characteristics of the mob—but that, under the circumstances, is also understandable. The audience understands Thomas instinctively. They know he is reaching out to them but cannot quite effect the meeting. The reaching ends in a tantalizing excitement, a frenzy. It is not a literary frenzy, the kind that ends in a riot with the police defending Edith Sitwell after a reading of *Façade*. On the contrary, it is the muttering of awakening, a slow realization about poetry, a totally unexpected apocalypse. This audience sees Thomas as a male Edna St. Vincent Millay, or perhaps a Charlie Chaplin; they hear the extraordinary vibrato, a voice of elation and anguish singing over their heads. They know it is acting. They know this is poetry and they know it is for them.

He is like the old cliché of vaudeville in which a tragicomic figure engaged in some private act (such as keeping his pants from falling down) wanders onto a stage where a highly formal cultural something is in progress. Naturally the embarrassed clown steals the show. One must remember Thomas's own story about himself in which he gets his finger stuck in a beer bottle. He goes from place to place, beer bottle and all, meeting new people. The beer bottle becomes Thomas's symbol of his natural self: it is his passport from the common people to the literary life, and back again. It is both his symbol of self and his symbol of other-self. But to Thomas it is mainly a horror symbol. It is the key to No Man's Land. Because Thomas is an uncivilizable Puritan and a hard-shell fundamentalist of some undefinable kind, the puritanism sets up the tension in his poetry—a tension based upon love and fear of love: the basic sexual tension, the basic theological tension. The greatness of Thomas is that he recognizes the equation; and the weakness of Thomas is that he takes to his heels when he has to grapple with it.

Everything I have said can be said better in the little poem by Thomas that takes nine lines. The last line of the poem is so much like a line of Whitman's that I have searched through Whitman's poems to find it. I am sure it is there and yet I know it isn't. The line reads "I advance for as long as forever is."

> Twenty-four years remind the tears of my eyes.
> (Bury the dead for fear that they walk to the grave in labour.)
> In the groin of the natural doorway I crouched like a tailor
> Sewing a shroud for a journey
> By the light of the meat-eating sun.
> Dressed to die, the sensual strut begun,
> With my red veins full of money,
> In the final direction of the elementary town
> I advance for as long as forever is.

Chronology of Important Dates

1914   Born October 27 in Swansea, South Wales.

1925-31   Educated at Swansea Grammar School.

1931-32   Proofreader and then apprentice reporter with the *South Wales Daily Post.*

1932-34   Amateur acting with the Swansea Little Theatre.

1933   May 18: First publication, "And death shall have no dominion," in the *New English Weekly.*

September 3: Prize poem "That Sanity Be Kept" published in the *Sunday Referee.*

1934   February 23: First trip to visit Pamela Hansford Johnson in London.

November 11: Moved to London.

December 18: *18 Poems* published by The Sunday Referee and the Parton Press.

1935   First meeting with Vernon Watkins.

Summer vacation with Geoffrey Grigson to west coast of Ireland.

1936   June-July: Visited International Surrealist Exhibition in New Burlington Galleries, London.

September: *Twenty-Five Poems* published by J. M. Dent and Sons.

1937   July 12: Married to Caitlin Macnamara at Penzance, Cornwall.

1937-38   Lived at Ringwood, Hampshire, and Sea View, Laugharne.

1939   January 30: First child, Llewelyn Thomas, born.

August 24: *The Map of Love.*

December 20: *The World I Breathe.*

1940   April 4: *Portrait of the Artist as a Young Dog.*

Rejected for military service. Moved first to Malting House, Wiltshire, and then to London.

1940-44   Working, mainly in London, for Donald Taylor, on scenarios for documentary films.

1943   March 3: Birth of Aeron Thomas, his second child.

1945   Moved to New Quay, Cardiganshire. Frequent broadcasts for B.B.C. throughout the next years.

1946   February 7: *Deaths and Entrances*.

        Moved to Oxford, helped by Mr. and Mrs. A. J. P. Taylor.

1947   Trip to Italy with Caitlin and family.

1948   Contract with Sydney Box to produce three scripts for feature-length films. The first was *Rebecca's Daughters*, an historical piece about Wales; the second was *The Beach of Falesá*, based on Robert Louis Stevenson's short story; and the third was a film operetta, *Me and My Bike*. None of these films were put into production at this time.

1949   Moved to the Boat House, Laugharne. Trip to Prague. July 24: Birth of Colm Thomas, his third child.

1950   February 21-May 31: First visit to America, after invitation by John Malcolm Brinnin. Readings at Poetry Center of the Young Men's and Women's Hebrew Association of New York, and at many American colleges.

        August 31: *Twenty-Six Poems*.

1952   January 20-May 16: Second visit to America.

        February 28: *In Country Sleep*.

        November 10: *Collected Poems*.

1953   April 21-June 3: Third visit to America.

        May: First performance of *Under Milk Wood* in Cambridge and New York.

        October 19: Fourth visit to America.

        November 9: Death in New York City.

        November 24: Burial in St. Martin's Churchyard, Laugharne.

Notes on the Editor and Authors

C. B. Cox, co-editor of *The Critical Quarterly*, is the author of *The Free Spirit: A Study of Liberal Humanism in the Novels of George Eliot, Henry James, E. M. Forster, Virginia Woolf and Angus Wilson*, and co-author with A. E. Dyson of *Modern Poetry: Studies in Practical Criticism* and *The Practical Criticism of Poetry*. He is Senior Lecturer in English at the University of Hull; during the year 1964-65 he was Visiting Associate Professor at the University of California, Berkeley.

JOHN WAIN, English novelist, critic and poet, works as a free-lance writer in Oxford.

DAVID DAICHES, well-known as the author of numerous books of literary criticism, is Dean of the School of English and American Studies at the University of Sussex.

JOHN ACKERMAN, poet and short story writer, is Lecturer in English, Avery Hill College of Education, London.

ELDER OLSON, poet and playwright, is Professor of English at the University of Chicago.

WINIFRED NOWOTTNY is Lecturer in English at University College, London.

RALPH MAUD, at present bringing out an edition of Dylan Thomas's early poetry notebooks, is Professor of English at Simon Fraser University, Burnaby, B.C., Canada.

WILLIAM EMPSON, famous poet and critic, is Professor of English at the University of Sheffield.

RAYMOND WILLIAMS, author of *Culture and Society, 1780-1950* and *The Long Revolution*, as well as other books of criticism and two novels, is Fellow of Jesus College, Cambridge, and Lecturer in English in the University of Cambridge.

DAVID HOLBROOK, author of two books of poetry, a collection of short stories, and several books on the teaching of English, is Fellow of King's College, Cambridge.

ANNIS PRATT studied at Columbia University under William York Tindall. She is a lecturer in English at Emory University in Atlanta, Georgia.

ROBERT M. ADAMS, author of books on Milton, Stendahl, and James Joyce, is Professor of English at Cornell University.

JOHN BAYLEY, author of *The Romantic Survival* and *The Characters of Love,* is Fellow of New College, Oxford, and lecturer in English in the University of Oxford.

KARL SHAPIRO, well-known poet and critic, is Professor of English at the University of Nebraska.

Selected Bibliography

Books by Dylan Thomas

18 Poems. London: The Sunday Referee and the Parton Press, 1934.

Twenty-Five Poems. London: J. M. Dent and Sons, 1936.

The Map of Love. London: J. M. Dent and Sons, 1939.

The World I Breathe. Norfolk, Conn.: New Directions, 1939.

Portrait of the Artist as a Young Dog. London: J. M. Dent and Sons, 1940.

New Poems. Norfolk, Conn.: New Directions, 1943.

Deaths and Entrances. London: J. M. Dent and Sons, 1946.

Selected Writings of Dylan Thomas. New York: New Directions, 1946.

Twenty-Six Poems. London: J. M. Dent and Sons, 1950.

In Country Sleep. New York: New Directions, 1952.

Collected Poems, 1934-1952. London: J. M. Dent and Sons, 1952.

The Doctor and the Devils. London: J. M. Dent and Sons, 1953.

Under Milk Wood. London: J. M. Dent and Sons, 1954.

Quite Early One Morning, Broadcasts. London: J. M. Dent and Sons, 1954.

Adventures in the Skin Trade and Other Stories. New York: New Directions, 1955.

A Prospect of the Sea. London: J. M. Dent and Sons, 1955.

A Child's Christmas in Wales. Norfolk, Conn.: New Directions, 1955.

Letters to Vernon Watkins. London: J. M. Dent and Sons and Faber and Faber, 1957.

The Beach of Falesá. New York: Stein and Day, 1963.

Twenty Years A-Growing (a film script from the story by Maurice O'Sullivan). London: J. M. Dent and Sons, 1964.

Select List of Books About Dylan Thomas

Ackerman, John. *Dylan Thomas, His Life and Work*. London: Oxford University Press, 1964.

Adams, Robert M. *Strains of Discord: Studies in Literary Openness*. Ithaca, New York: Cornell University Press, 1958.

Bayley, John. *The Romantic Survival*. London: Constable and Co., 1957.

Brinnin, John Malcolm, ed. *A Casebook on Dylan Thomas.* New York: Thomas Y. Crowell, 1960.

Brinnin, John Malcolm. *Dylan Thomas in America.* Boston: Little, Brown and Co., 1955.

Daiches, David. *Literary Essays.* Edinburgh: Oliver and Boyd, 1956.

Fitzgibbon, Constantine. *The Life of Dylan Thomas.* London: J. M. Dent and Sons, 1965.

Fraser, G. S. *Dylan Thomas.* London: Longmans Green and Company, 1957.

Holbrook, David. *Llareggub Revisited: Dylan Thomas and the State of Modern Poetry.* London: Bowes and Bowes, 1962. Reprinted as *Dylan Thomas and Poetic Dissociation.* Carbondale: Southern Illinois University Press, 1964.

Jones, T. H. *Dylan Thomas.* Edinburgh: Oliver and Boyd, 1963.

Kleinman, Hyman H. *The Religious Sonnets of Dylan Thomas: A Study in Imagery and Meaning.* Berkeley: University of California Press, 1963.

Maud, Ralph, and Aneirin T. Davies, eds. *The Colour of Saying: An Anthology of Verse Spoken by Dylan Thomas.* London: J. M. Dent and Sons, 1963.

Maud, Ralph. *Entrances to Dylan Thomas' Poetry.* Pittsburgh, Pa.: University of Pittsburgh Press, 1963.

Nowottny, Winifred. *The Language Poets Use.* London: The Athlone Press, 1962.

Olson, Elder. *The Poetry of Dylan Thomas.* Chicago: University of Chicago Press, 1954.

Read, Bill, and Rollie McKenna. *The Days of Dylan Thomas.* New York: McGraw-Hill Book Company, 1964.

Rolph, J. Alexander. *Dylan Thomas: A Bibliography.* London: J. M. Dent and Sons, 1956.

Scarfe, Francis. *Auden and After.* London: Routledge and Sons, 1942.

Shapiro, Karl. *In Defense of Ignorance.* New York: Random House, 1960.

Stanford, Derek. *Dylan Thomas.* London: Neville Spearman, 1954.

Tedlock, E. W., ed. *Dylan Thomas: The Legend and the Poet.* London: William Heinemann, 1960.

Thomas, Caitlin. *Leftover Life to Kill.* London: Putnam and Co., 1957.

Tindall, W. Y. *A Reader's Guide to Dylan Thomas.* New York: Farrar, Straus and Company, 1962.

Treece, Henry. *Dylan Thomas: Dog Among the Fairies.* London: Lindsay Drummond, 1949. Rev. ed., London: Ernest Benn, 1959.